THE BOYS NEXT DOOR

A PLAY IN TWO ACTS
BY TOM GRIFFIN

D0067340

DRAMATISTS
PLAY SERVICE
INC.

THE BOYS NEXT DOOR
Copyright © 1988, Tom Griffin
Copyright © 1983, Tom Griffin
under the title "Damaged Hearts, Broken Flowers"

All Rights Reserved

SPECIAL NOTE

SPECIAL NOTE ON SONGS AND RECORDINGS

THE BOYS NEXT DOOR, the Berkshire Theatre Festival production, was presented by Jay H. Fuchs and Joseph Tandet in association with Sports Entertainment Group and Little Prince Productions Ltd. at the Lamb's Theatre in New York City on November 23, 1987. It was directed by Josephine R. Abady; the scenery was by David Potts; the costumes were by C. L. Hundley; the lighting was by Michael Chybowski; the sound design was by Lia Vollack; the hair design was by Marcia Ann Ames; the casting was by Pat McCorkle; the associate producer was Robin Benson Fuchs; and the production stage manager was Peggy Peterson. The cast, in order of appearance, was as follows:

ARNOLD WIGGINS................... Joe Grifasi
LUCIEN P. SMITH....................William Jay
JACK.......................... Dennis Boutsikaris
NORMAN BULANSKY................ Josh Mostel
BARRY KLEMPER...................... Joe Urla
MR. HEDGES, MR. CORBIN, SENATOR CLARKE
....John Wylie
MRS. FREMUS, MRS. WARREN, CLARA
.... Laurinda Barrett
SHEILA...................... Christine Estabrook
MR. KLEMPER...................... Ed Setrakian

THE BOYS NEXT DOOR was originally produced by the McCarter Theatre Company, Princeton, New Jersey, in June, 1986.

CHARACTERS

Arnold Wiggins
Lucien P. Smith
Norman Bulansky
Barry Klemper
Jack
Sheila
Mr. Klemper

The play has been designed so that the following roles may be played by one actress and one actor:

Mrs. Fremus
Mrs. Warren
Clara
Mr. Hedges
Mr. Corbin
Senator Clarke

Note: Neither Sheila nor Mr. Klemper should ever be double-cast.

Time: The present. Summer.

Place: New England.

A modest two-bedroom apartment in a large apartment complex. The area is suburban.

Setting: The play is divided into scenes; however, the main setting is the living room of the apartment and the adjacent efficiency kitchen. It is a rather unimaginatively designed and decorated space. The kitchen area has the usuals: stove, refrigerator, sink, cabinets, small breakfast table, et al. The main room has a couch, chairs, an end table or two, lamps, a coffee table, and bland retail art on the walls. It is neither neat nor sloppy, but it is certainly lived in. There is "stuff" around and "things" about.

Arnold, Norman, Lucien, and Barry live here.

There are four entrances to the room:
A door to the bathroom.
A door to Norman and Arnold's bedroom.
A door to Barry and Lucien's bedroom.
A front door which leads to the apartment hallway, maybe even an outdoor walkway.

The other scenes take place in a variety of placcs. All are suggested with lighting, location, props, and set pieces.

THE BOYS NEXT DOOR

SUMMER. The apartment. Arnold Wiggins is sitting.
On the floor are four supermarket bags. The contents are
undisclosed.
Arnold is a very nervous man in his forties. He wears
nondescript summer clothing.

ARNOLD. (*Directly to the audience.*) My name is Arnold Wiggins. I'm basically a nervous person. People call me Arnold because I don't have a nickname. So I pretend that Arnold is my nickname so that when people call me Arnold, I pretend that they are close personal friends who know me by my nickname: Arnold. I live here at the Stonehenge Villa apartment complex in a group apartment with three other guys. Did I mention I'm a nervous person? Well, frankly, I am. Today I went to the market at the end of the street to get some Wheaties. But I couldn't remember whether I wanted one box or more boxes, so I asked the manager how many boxes I should get. "For just you?" he said. "Yes, sir," I said. "Seventeen," he said. "Thank you," I said. But, and this is what I want to emphasize by nervous, I could only find nine boxes. So what could I do? (*Pause.*) I got nine boxes of Wheaties. (*He removes various sized boxes of Wheaties from the bags.*) And seven heads of lettuce. (*He removes the lettuce, studies the situation.*) That made sixteen. (*Pulls out a bag of charcoal.*) And one bag of charcoal briquets. That made seventeen. (*He takes out the milk.*) And a quart of milk. You know, for the Wheaties. But the more I thought about it, the more I thought I didn't get enough . . . what? Was it (A) lettuce? (B) Wheaties? (C) charcoal briquets? This concerned me. So I asked a girl in line what she thought. I forget what she said, but it was pretty thorough. And then I came home. (*Pause.*)

Do you think I did the right thing? (*Lucien enters from his bedroom. He carries a stack of library books. Lucien P. Smith is a large black man of about fifty. He is quite slow. He dresses simply. He sees the lettuce, Wheaties, et al.*)

LUCIEN. What's them?

ARNOLD. (*Defensively.*) Just stuff I got at the market. We were running a little low. (*Lucien puts down the books and pulls from his pocket a worn library card.*)

LUCIEN. I got this. See it.

ARNOLD. It's your library card. It's nice.

LUCIEN. It says my name.

ARNOLD. Lucien Smith. I see it right there.

LUCIEN. It be green.

ARNOLD. It's nice.

LUCIEN. Lucien P. Smith.

ARNOLD. Libraries have that funny smell.

LUCIEN. It smells like books.

ARNOLD. That's it. Books. They smell like books.

LUCIEN. (*Examining the lettuce.*) Bunnies like lettuce.

ARNOLD. Yes, they constantly do. (*With suspicion.*) Do you have a bunny?

LUCIEN. You got a bunny hid?

ARNOLD. No, really, Lucien, you never mentioned a bunny before. This concerns me a little. I mean, we're friends and all, and you've never said nothing about a bunny.

LUCIEN. It's got my name. Lucien P. Smith. (*Indicating the books.*) You read them.

ARNOLD. Sure. But I repeat, I have not forgot the bunny. (*Reading the spines of the books.*) Department of Agriculture Yearbook — 1947.

LUCIEN. Lucien P. Smith like hard books. It's hard.

ARNOLD. *Department of Agriculture Yearbook — 1948. Department of Agriculture Yearbook — 1950.*

LUCIEN. It be a set.

ARNOLD. *Department of Agriculture Yearbook — 1951. Department of Agriculture Yearbook — 1952. Department of Agriculture Yearbook — 1949.*

LUCIEN. Hard, hard, hard.

ARNOLD. *Department of Agriculture Yearbook — 1955.*

LUCIEN. Pretty good, huh? Where's the bunny hid?

ARNOLD. Did you lose a bunny? Now tell me the truth, Lucien. This is really beginning to bother me.

LUCIEN. I be reading good now. (*Sings "The Alphabet Song."*)* "A B C D . . . L MNOP . . ."

ARNOLD. No, listen, Lucien. This has to be emphasized. I've got (A) Wheaties, (B) lettuce, and (C) charcoal briquets.

LUCIEN. "F . . . L M N O P . . ."

ARNOLD. And a quart of milk for the Wheaties. Did I mention the Wheaties? I think I forgot the Wheaties. Okay, so let's say the Wheaties are (D). You follow me, right? The Wheaties are (D).

LUCIEN. (*Still lightly.*) "L M N O P . . . Z . . ."

ARNOLD. So I've got (A) charcoal briquets, (B) lettuce, (C) Wheaties, and (D) Wheaties. Something is screwed up here.

LUCIEN. It's a hard song. (*The doorbell rings.*)

ARNOLD. It must be the door!

LUCIEN. (*Indicating the bags et al.*) What about them? You can get in trouble. Jack'd be mad.

ARNOLD. (*Suddenly panicky.*) I know. I don't know . . . I don't know . . .

LUCIEN. (*Stuffing the briquets up his shirt front.*) I got this.

ARNOLD. I know. I've got it!

LUCIEN. (*His shirt now bulging.*) I got this.

ARNOLD. The tub. We'll put it all in the tub. (*Chanting.*) In the tub. In the tub. In the tub. In the tub.

LUCIEN. (*Gathering lettuce.*) In the tub. In the tub. In the tub.

ARNOLD. (*Gathering Wheaties.*) In the tub! In the tub! In the tub!

LUCIEN. In the tub! In the tub! In the tub!

ARNOLD. In the tub! In the tub! (*The doorbell rings again.*) Stop! (*A brilliant idea.*) I'd better get the door first.

LUCIEN. Get the door. Get the door. Get the door.

ARNOLD. I'll get the door, then we'll put it in the tub. Okay?

LUCIEN. (*Struggling with the lettuce.*) Get the door! Get the door! Get the door!

---

*See Special Note on Copyright page.

ARNOLD. C'mon, Lucien! Okay?

LUCIEN. I'll just be standing.

ARNOLD. (*The great conspirator.*) This is perfect, Lucien. Perfect. I'll get the door. Don't give it away.

LUCIEN. I'll just be standing.

ARNOLD. This is beautiful! (*Arnold, still clutching a few boxes of Wheaties, opens the front door. Jack Palmer stands there. He is a wry man in his mid-thirties. He carries a grocery bag. As Jack sees Lucien, Lucien drops the heads of lettuce. Lucien and Arnold exchange a look. Jack enters, quickly surveying the situation.*) Hi, Jack. It's nice to see you, Jack.

LUCIEN. It's a nice day today.

ARNOLD. It's a real beautiful day, Jack, isn't it?

LUCIEN. Nice day.

ARNOLD. Not too many clouds in the sky today.

LUCIEN. Not too many . . . bunnies in the sky today. It's nice.

JACK. You're right, Lucien. I drove all the way over here and not one bunny. (*Removing a box of Wheaties from his grocery bag.*) So, what are you two guys up to?

ARNOLD. Just hanging around.

LUCIEN. Hanging around.

JACK. That's a good thing to do on a Saturday. Saturday is a good hang around day. What's that up your shirt, Lucien?

LUCIEN. My shirt?

JACK. Yeah. There's something up your shirt. At least I hope there's something up your shirt.

ARNOLD. (*Improvising.*) He had a big breakfast.

LUCIEN. My breakfast. It be big.

ARNOLD. Bacon, French toast, juice, sausage, orange juice, pie. Bacon. Did I say bacon?

LUCIEN. And bacon too.

ARNOLD. Pancakes, waffles, eggs, bacon, potatoes, cheese, toast . . .

LUCIEN. (*Blurting.*) In the tub! In the tub! In the tub!

ARNOLD. Not now, Lucien! Not yet! (*Norman Bulansky enters by the front door. Fat and sloppy and maybe thirty, Norman wears a doughnut shop uniform, replete with trim. There is a large overflowing key ring on his belt. He is obviously concealing something beneath his shirt: a doughnut box. He begins speaking with a burst the moment the door opens.*)

10

NORMAN. Oh boy! The bus sure was crowded. Oh boy, I had to sit up front with old people. You get a real good look out the windows if you sit with the old people. One of those old people said, "How are you today?" Oh boy! I hate those questions. (*Spotting the Wheaties.*) Who's Wheaties?

ARNOLD. You had to mention it, didn't you? You couldn't just ignore them, could you? You couldn't just ignore.

NORMAN. I'm sorry, Arnold. Honest. I'm sorry.

ARNOLD. You worry me, Norman. Honestly, you cause me serious concern.

JACK. Hi, Norman

NORMAN. Oh, Jack. Hi, Jack. How are you? The job's going great. Nice to see you. (*An obvious faked yawn.*) Well, I'd better get to bed. I'm real sleepy. That bus, oh boy, was it ever crowded. I had to sit up front with the old people. I need a good night's sleep. So, good night everyone. Come again. (*Norman starts for his bedroom, still concealing the box. As he does so, Arnold surreptitiously stuffs a box of Wheaties beneath his own shirt.*)

JACK. Norman.

NORMAN. (*Yawning and stretching.*) These late hours, oh boy, they really get a man tired.

JACK. It's early afternoon, Norman.

NORMAN. It is?

JACK. What's that under your shirt, Norman?

NORMAN. Under my shirt?

JACK. Under your shirt. This is beginning to become an epidemic.

NORMAN. Oh boy! Do I have something under my shirt? I'm really glad you told me. What could it be?

JACK. The suspense is killing us.

NORMAN. (*Taking out the doughnut box, with exaggerated surprise.*) Doughnuts? Oh boy! I didn't even notice. Doughnuts!

LUCIEN. (*Proudly, as if in a contest, taking out the briquets.*) I got charcoal briquets!

ARNOLD. I don't believe this. You make a plan, you think it all through, you work out all the details, and then . . . I'll tell you truthfully, I really don't believe this. This is the kind of thing that bothers me a lot. I mean, it was foolproof.

(*Arnold, Lucien, and Norman sit. Lucien has the briquets. Norman has the doughnuts. Arnold still has the Wheaties.*)

JACK. (*To the audience.*) My name is Jack Palmer. For the past eight months I've been supervising five group apartments of the mentally handicapped. Seventeen adult men. The idea is to introduce them into the mainstream (*Pause.*) Most of the time, I laugh at their escapades. But sometimes the laughter wears thin. The truth is they're burning me out. (*A beat.*) But, somehow, despite this, they remain my closest associates. (*Amidst the men.*) At the doughnut shop where Norman works, his nickname is Billy Bulemia. At the end of the shift, they gather all the broken doughnuts and give them to Norman. This is construed as an act of kindness by both Norman and the people at the doughnut shop. Since Norman started working there three months ago, he's gained seventeen pounds. And Lucien, on a recent group trip to a local petting zoo, stunned a host of schoolchildren and toddlers by climbing atop an apathetic cow and yelling loudly, "Fire! This cow be on fire!" Two weeks ago, Arnold bought a weather radio. After four days of nothing but weather, Arnold called the Coast Guard and informed them there was a plot to suppress music, news, and commercials. And finally, Barry, who you've not yet met, has convinced himself that he's a golf pro. He even put up a sign in the recreation room of the apartment complex advertising private lessons. At a dollar thirteen an hour. At last count, he had four pupils signed up. So, my question is, "Who's on first?" (*The men remain in the apartment as the lights fade. Barry and Mr. Hedges on the grounds of the apartment complex. A bench. Bright sun. Mr. Hedges holds a six iron. Barry Klemper is twenty-eight. He wears a pastel "golf outfit" and sneakers. He is full of positive conviction.*)

BARRY. I'll tell you one of the basic problems of golf. Maybe the basic problem of golf. Golf is a game. It's just a game, Mr. Hodges, just a game.

MR. HEDGES. Hedges.

BARRY. It's too early to worry about that. Besides, I don't know of more than two or three courses with a serious hedge hazard. Sure, traps. Sure, thick rough. Sure. But hedges. That's rare.

MR. HEDGES. My name is Hedges. My name is John Hedges.

BARRY. I have no reason to doubt that. But you're paying good money for this lesson, and we can't spend all the time worrying about the occasional hedge. It just doesn't make sense.

MR. HEDGES. Are you joking?

BARRY. I don't joke, John. (*Pause.*) Today, our first lesson, we're not even going to touch a club. Please put your club down.

MR. HEDGES. I'm just holding it.

BARRY. Please.

MR. HEDGES. (*Warily putting down the club.*) Sure. Right.

BARRY. Thank you. Now the first lesson, today's lesson, I call, "How To Handle a Heckler in the Gallery."

MR. HEDGES. Gallery? What gallery? I play on a nine hole public course. I just want a few basic tips.

BARRY. The pros always have a crowd. Always a gallery. Aspire, Mr. Hodges, aspire to be a champion.

MR. HEDGES. Hedges.

BARRY. (*Frustrated.*) Hedges! Golf is more than hedges, Hodges. Golf is the little things. The basics. Execution. Execution. Execution.

MR. HEDGES. (*Also frustrated.*) All right, fine, give me a basic. Just give me one basic.

BARRY. What you want is a tip, a golf tip, something that'll help you right now. Am I right?

MR. HEDGES. Yes. That's what I want.

BARRY. Fine. Let me take a moment.

MR. HEDGES. Maybe we should just forget this whole thing. It doesn't seem to be working out.

BARRY. Don't quit now, John. Hang in there. I know that the first lesson is difficult, but it'll get easier. I promise you. There'll be a lot less to memorize as we go along.

MR. HEDGES. (*Now coldly.*) What's the tip?

BARRY. Okay. Let me think. There are so many. Ah, here's one that I think can be quite useful. At the top of your backswing, come to a complete stop, the club parallel to the ground, and take a moment to reflect on how fortunate we

13

are to live in a time when golf is in full flower. Then hit that little round sucker as viciously as you can. (*The lights fade and come up on the apartment. Lucien gets up and gathers his library books.*)

LUCIEN. I'm gonna be go looking at my books. They're hard. I be doing it alone.

JACK. Looks like some pretty serious reading there, Lucien.

LUCIEN. Hard, hard, hard.

ARNOLD. It's agriculture.

NORMAN. At the doughnut shop, I saw this book in the men's room. Oh boy! Whew!

ARNOLD. You have to study agriculture in a set. Year by year. Otherwise, it won't make any sense.

NORMAN. There were girls in there with, oh boy, nothing on. I mean, oh boy, nothing.

LUCIEN. It be a set.

ARNOLD. Nothing? You mean nothing?

NORMAN. One girl was in the snow. She had nothing on.

ARNOLD. In the snow? With nothing on? In the snow? With nothing on?

JACK. Yes, Arnold, she was in the snow with nothing on. Do you think maybe we could zoom in on the problem of the Wheaties?

NORMAN. She had a hat.

LUCIEN. Where's the bunny?

ARNOLD. Jack, he's been doing this all day. About a million times. And he won't give out any information. I'll catch angina if he keeps it up.

NORMAN. And she had those big giant shoes like big pans.

ARNOLD. See, it's true. There was a girl with nothing on with giant shoes and a hat out in the snow and I'm the last to know.

JACK. Arnold, I want you to take all this stuff back to the store.

ARNOLD. You're just changing the subject because of that girl in the snow. It's a trick.

LUCIEN. It's hard. (*Lucien exits into his bedroom with the library books.*)

JACK. I've told you over and over not to buy stuff at Livingston's Market. I've told you they take advantage of you. I've told you they . . . tease you. I've done the whole bit, but nothing works. So, we're going to try yet another approach.

ARNOLD. This is very nerve-wracking, Jack.

JACK. I want you to take the Wheaties and the lettuce and the milk and the charcoal and put them back in their bags and take the bags and put them back in the shopping cart and take it all back.

ARNOLD. Take it all back where?

JACK. To Livingston's Market. And I want you to tell the manager that you want your money back. Have you got a receipt?

ARNOLD. It's in one of the bags.

JACK. Fine.

ARNOLD. I don't like this. I don't like this at all.

NORMAN. I get to keep the doughnuts, right?

JACK. No, you do not get to keep the doughnuts. Now, listen, Arnold, just tell the manager you want your money back. Okay?

ARNOLD. I don't know, Jack. I mean, that's pretty embarrassing.

JACK. I know it's tough, Arnold, but you can do it. (*Sees Norman sneaking a doughnut.*) Norman, if you take one bite of that doughnut, I'm going to take all your keys and have them melted down into a lawn statue.

NORMAN. (*Guarding the overflowing key ring on his belt.*) I need my keys. They're important. I can't . . . get into things without my keys.

JACK. It's your decision, Norman. Your doughnuts or your keys. Take your time.

NORMAN. Can I eat while I'm thinking it over?

ARNOLD. (*Heading for his bedroom.*) It's a good idea, Jack. I'm going to put it right down on my list of things to do.

JACK. Stop right there. And no, Norman, you cannot eat while you think it over. And Arnold, you are going to do it now.

ARNOLD. Now?

JACK. (*Loading stuff in the bags.*) I'll even help you with the bags. C'mon. Now.

NORMAN. I need my keys.

JACK. Don't forget the briquets.

NORMAN. There's a blueberry one in here. It has a bite out of it, but it's still good.

ARNOLD. (*A brilliant idea.*) I can't do it! I don't know the manager's name. There. That's final.

JACK. Now. (*Sees Norman with a doughnut.*) If you don't put that down, Norman, your keys are ancient history. (*Norman relents. Arnold takes two bags and starts for the front door.*)

ARNOLD. I just want you to know that in my entire life I have never seen such pressure. This is like Russia around here. Boy, a guy can't even eat a doughnut or get a few things in for a rainy day. Boy! (*Arnold exits with the bags.*)

NORMAN. He's mad. (*Heading for the kitchen.*) I'll put these in the refrigerator. You know, for later.

JACK. Just for a snack, right?

NORMAN. Yeah. You know, for later.

JACK. What about that girl you like? That one that goes to the Wednesday night dances? What do you think she'd think?

NORMAN. (*Affected.*) What girl?

JACK. You know what girl. Sheila.

NORMAN. Sheila. She's nice. I like her.

JACK. Didn't she say you were too fat? (*No response.*) And didn't you tell me that you were going to stop eating all these doughnuts? Come on now, Norman. (*Arnold enters. Grouchily, he gets another bag.*)

ARNOLD. Maybe I'll just move to Russia, I repeat, to Russia. Maybe I'll just pack all my things and move there. You know, I think I will. That's a good idea. I'll just take all my stuff to Russia. (*Jack and Norman watch as Arnold again exits.*)

NORMAN. He's mad. (*An embarrassed pause.*) Sheila doesn't like fast dances. She likes slow dances. You know what she did?

JACK. What?

NORMAN. Right in the middle of this real fast dance, she stopped. Like when the bus stops. Oh boy! I thought she was broken or something.

JACK. (*Gently.*) That kind of thing happens all the time.

NORMAN. That's what I figured. You know, who can keep up with it? (*Arnold enters again and gets the final bag.*)

ARNOLD. My mind is made up. Nobody can talk me out of

it. I'm moving to Russia tomorrow, thank you very much. (*Arnold exits.*)

JACK & NORMAN. (*Together.*) He's mad.

NORMAN. (*Giving Jack the doughnuts.*) Jack, you have them.

JACK. I'm proud of you, Norman.

NORMAN. She's not no Skinny Minnie herself. (*With hesitation.*) Can I take her here some time?

JACK. Sure, Norman, we'll have Harry and the van pick her up some day.

NORMAN. With just me and her? Here alone?

JACK. Alone? I don't know, Norman. Alone is kind of against the rules.

NORMAN. She's not so Skinny Minnie herself. (*Pause.*) I love her and pretty soon we're gonna get married and have one baby boy and one baby girl. And we're gonna always take the baby boy and the baby girl everyplace we go. That's a law we made. Everyplace. Even if Sheila and me have to go in the army or something. (*Norman exits happily into his bedroom.*)

JACK. (*To the audience.*) If Norman joins the army, and Arnold moves to Russia, and Barry goes on the Pro Tour, and Lucien gives his life to agriculture, I'll have a lot more free time. (*A moment.*) Lucien and Norman are retarded. Arnold is marginal. A depressive by trade, he will fool you sometimes, but his deck has no face cards. Barry, on the other hand, really doesn't belong here in the first place. He's a grade A schizophrenic with a chronic history of institutions. Loony, teetering on the edge, but clearly resourceful, Barry tells all his problems to Mrs. Fremus, the deaf widow three apartments down. She knits. He talks. I call it Madame De-Farge and The Golf Pro. (*Jack exits by the front door. Mrs. Fremus' porch. Barry and Mrs. Fremus are sitting. She knits. Barry is wearing his pastel golf outfit. Mrs. Fremus is in dark, almost funereal colors.*)

BARRY. I couldn't begin to figure it. He just quit. Hodges quit. He was obsessed with hedges. He walked away screaming at me, "Hedges! Hedges! Hedges!" Now I'm down to two students. I figured it out. At one dollar and thirteen cents per student, each student would have to take forty hours of instruction each week just for me to get ninety dollars and

17

forty cents. I computed it. That's before expenses. (*Dawns on him.*) I still have to buy clubs yet.

MRS. FREMUS. You don't need gloves in the summer, Barry.

BARRY. (*Highly agitated.*) "Clubs!" I said. Clubs! (*Moonlight seeps into the darkened apartment. The beam from a large flashlight emerges from the bathroom. Lucien, dressed in a pair of worn pajamas, pops his head out and calls for the others.*)

LUCIEN. (*In a loud whisper.*) Guys! Guys! I got him! He be trapped! (*Arnold and Norman emerge from each of the bedrooms. They also have lit flashlights. Norman is in his underwear. His keys dangle from an improvised belt. He wields a pillow. Arnold wears pajamas with large bedroom slippers. He carries a large aluminum bowl.*)

NORMAN. (*Loudly.*) Where is he!

ARNOLD. Sssshhhh . . .

LUCIEN. Guys! He's caught! He be trapped! Under the toilet!

ARNOLD. Sssshhhh!

LUCIEN. He's big! He be a big one!

ARNOLD. Sssssshhhhh!!! (*Norman turns on the main light switch. Lucien, his flashlight in one hand and a heavy sponge mop in the other, stands at the opened bathroom door. Panicky.*) Norman, what are you doing? Are you crazy? Now he can see!

NORMAN. I thought it'd be better.

ARNOLD. Don't you understand? Rats can't see in the dark. It's a behavior pattern. They can't see in the dark!

LUCIEN. He be trapped.

ARNOLD. The door's open!

LUCIEN. The rat be trapped.

ARNOLD. Shut the door! No! No, wait. We need a plan. We need an airtight plan. Rats are sneaky. That's why everybody says, "You sneaky rat." We can't waste any time. Norman, shut off the lights. First thing, we'll blind him. Go on, shut 'em off! (*Norman shuts off the lights. The flashlights still glow.*) Now, Lucien, count to three, then shut the door. Very easy. Don't let him know where you are.

LUCIEN. I be home.

ARNOLD. I know where you are. Don't let the rat know where you are.

18

NORMAN. Tell him you're not home.
LUCIEN. I be not home!
ARNOLD. Shut the door!
LUCIEN. There he goes! There he goes! There he goes!
(*Lucien, flashlight blazing, runs for the kitchen. The men follow. Confusion and hubbub.*)
ARNOLD. I told you to shut the door!
NORMAN. I see him! I see him!
ARNOLD. Get him! Hit him! Pounce on him!
NORMAN. I see him!
LUCIEN. (*Yelling.*) I be not home! (*Norman pounces on the rat with the pillow. Lucien pounds both the pillow and Norman. Groans and confusion.*)
NORMAN. I got him! I got him!
LUCIEN. I be not home! I be not home!
ARNOLD. Did you get him?
NORMAN. I got him!
LUCIEN. We got him!
ARNOLD. I'll get the lights. (*Turns on the lights.*) Now check him out. Did you get him?
NORMAN. (*Peeking under his pillow.*) He's still moving!
ARNOLD. Get him! Smother him!
LUCIEN. (*Pounding the pillow.*) I be not home! I be not home! I be not home!
NORMAN. (*Jumping on the pillow.*) Smother the rat! Smother the rat! Smother the rat!
ARNOLD. Stop! (*They do so.*) Check him out.
NORMAN. (*Again looking.*) We got him. We got the rat.
LUCIEN. We got the rat.
ARNOLD. Okay, now quick, let me think. Where can we put him?
LUCIEN. I be bury him in the sandbox.
ARNOLD. You can't bury him in the sandbox, Lucien. The kids play in the sandbox. You can't bury rats where kids play.
LUCIEN. How come?
ARNOLD. Because you can't. It's unsanitary.
NORMAN. We have this thing at the doughnut shop. All you do is put your hands under it. It's red lights. It kills all the germs.
ARNOLD. Let me think. I've got it. The toilet. We'll flush him down.

19

LUCIEN. Rats, they swim.

ARNOLD. Ssshhh!!! Let me think. (*Pause.*) Okay, we'll flush him down the toilet. But first, just in case, we'll turn off the lights. (*He turns off the lights.*) Okay, now he's blinded. Get him by the tail and bring him in the bathroom. Lucien, you flush. I'll stand watch at the door.

NORMAN. By the tail?

ARNOLD. By the tail!

NORMAN. (*Studying the rat with his flashlight.*) It's small.

LUCIEN. Maybe he be sleeping.

ARNOLD. Pick him up. You got him?

NORMAN. (*With the rat.*) He don't weigh much.

ARNOLD. Go on. Take him. Take him. (*Norman, Lucien, and the rat all start for the bathroom. The front door opens. Light streams in. Barry, dressed in a jogging outfit, enters.*)

BARRY. Who turned off the lights?

ARNOLD. Ssshhh . . . We caught a rat.

NORMAN. Hi, Barry. It's nice to see you.

LUCIEN. I got the rat.

NORMAN. But I can't see you.

ARNOLD. We're going to flush him. (*Barry turns on the lights.*) Turn 'em off! Turn 'em off!

BARRY. This is my place too and I don't intend to spend all night in the dark.

ARNOLD. Norman, hurry, flush him! (*Norman and Lucien rush into the bathroom. They flush the rat. Barry, seemingly exhausted, flops into a chair. Norman and Lucien emerge from the bathroom, triumphant.*)

LUCIEN. We did it!

NORMAN. He went down just like toilet paper. Whew! Oh boy.

ARNOLD. I'll get the lights. (*Arnold shuts off the lights.*)

LUCIEN. Lucien P. Smith be tired.

NORMAN. It just sucked him right down.

ARNOLD. That's one of the bravest things I've ever done.

LUCIEN. Hi, Barry. It's a nice day today.

BARRY. (*From the darkness.*) The Crosley kid quit today. Right in the middle of the lesson. "I'm only nine years old," the Crosley kid said. "So what?" I said. "I'm twenty-eight."

Now I'm down to just one pupil. It was a great lesson too. I called it, "The Dos and Don'ts of Renting a Golf Cart." I had pictures and everything. It really irks me. All these people ever want to do is golf. (*The apartment goes to black. A railroad siding. Bright sun. Muted train sounds. Jack has a deli sandwich and juice.*)

JACK. (*To the audience.*) Sometimes, I eat lunch down here by the railroad tracks. It's very romantic in a sordid kind of way. (*Pause.*) I ran into my ex-wife the other day. She's full of ex-whatever venom. She asked me a few polite questions about my job, then she said, "What happens when they don't need you any more?" "They'll never not need me any more," I told her. "Me or somebody else." "Who made that rule?" she asked. "God," I said. (*Pause.*) Three months ago, Lucien was informed by the Social Security Administration that his benefits were being cut off. They said that their information indicated that Lucien was capable of being fully integrated into the community. We appealed. No luck. Our next step is to appear before a State Senate subcommittee. Lucien has been invited as a witness. I try to prepare him, but I don't think it's taking. He says if he knows "The Alphabet Song," it'll be okay. He says he wants to wear a tie with Spiderman on it. Just so they'll know how important this is. (*Pause.*) And as a final note, my ex-wife looked terrific. She drives a BMW now and wears lots of bright green. "Who's that funny little man in the back seat of your car?" she asked me. It was Arnold. "That's Arnold," I said. "Why is he reading the phone book sideways?" she said. "He's looking for the road map to Russia," I said. "How can you stand it?" she said. And Arnold, still in the back seat of the car, said, "If the phone people don't want to print maps of Russia, fine. But don't turn around and call it the phone book. Don't deceive the public." (*The scene switches to Arnold. He wheels a shopping cart. An inexplicable small shrub sits in the cart. He stops.*)

ARNOLD. (*To the audience.*) When I went back to Livingston's Market to get my money back, the manager called me "a fucking nut." So I called him a banana republic. (*Pause.*) Did I get even or what? (*Morning in the apartment. Bright sun*

comes in the windows. Barry, in golf clothes, sits drinking orange juice and perusing the "Wall Street Journal." Lucien, in his pajamas, watches.)
LUCIEN. Barry?
BARRY. Yeah.
LUCIEN. Maybe I can golf.
BARRY. Yeah?
LUCIEN. I killed the rat.
BARRY. Killing rats and golfing are two different sports, Lucien.
LUCIEN. Oh . . . The funnies, can I see it?
BARRY. This is the *Wall Street Journal.* There are no funnies in this paper.
LUCIEN. How come?
BARRY. This is a businessman's paper. There's no room in a businessman's paper for funnies.
LUCIEN. You be a business now, huh, Barry?
BARRY. I might even rent a beeper. I'm looking into it. You better get dressed. When Harry comes with the van, he'll be pissed if you aren't ready. Work is work, Lucien. You think a guy learns to play his sand shots in his pajamas. Not in this league.
LUCIEN. I could golf.
BARRY. Everybody thinks they can golf, Lucien. That's why there's golf courses.
LUCIEN. Can I see the funnies?
BARRY. There are no funnies in this paper.
LUCIEN. Can I see it then?
BARRY. See what?
LUCIEN. Snoopy.
BARRY. *(Frustrated.)* There are no funnies. There is no Snoopy. This is the *Wall Street Journal!*
LUCIEN. *(After a moment.)* I be getting dressed.
BARRY. And if I get a beeper, I'm the only one that's going to be allowed to touch it. Beepers aren't toys. They're tools of industry. *(Norman enters. He carries mail. He wears his doughnut shop uniform, complete with keys.)*
NORMAN. I just said to Mrs. Fremus, "It's a nice day today." She said, "I never drink iced tea." Oh boy, did that throw me. What do you think she meant?

22

BARRY. She's a very intelligent woman, Norman. Sometimes I don't get her gist at first, but it always sinks in after a while.

NORMAN. You got mail. (*Handing Barry the mail.*) A golf book and a letter.

BARRY. A letter?

LUCIEN. Snoopy, he golfs.

BARRY. I told you to get dressed.

NORMAN. (*Mulling it over.*) "I never drink iced tea . . . I never drink iced tea . . ."

LUCIEN. Me neither. I be getting dressed. (*Lucien exits into his bedroom. Norman stands over Barry as Barry reads the letter.*)

NORMAN. Who's it from? (*No response.*) Can I have the stamp when you're done? (*No response.*) Is it a golf letter?

BARRY. (*After a pause, affected.*) It's from . . . my Dad. He's coming to visit me. He's going to be in Boston for a day and he's coming down to visit me.

NORMAN. Are you done with the stamp? (*Barry silently gets up, shaken by the letter. He starts for the bathroom.*)

BARRY. He's going to be in Boston and he says he's coming down to visit me. (*The front doorbell rings.*)

NORMAN. He's here! Oh boy, he's fast.

BARRY. (*Trancelike.*) It's from Dad . . . My Dad . . . Dad is coming to visit me . . . (*Clutching the letter, Barry exits into the bathroom. The doorbell rings again. Norman looks around somewhat helplessly. He starts for the front door.*)

NORMAN. (*Calling in to Barry.*) I'll tell your Dad you're in the bathroom! (*Norman opens the door. Mrs. Warren stands there. She is a cheerful woman in her thirties.*)

MRS. WARREN. Hello.

NORMAN. (*By rote.*) Hello. My name is Norman Bulansky. Welcome to my home. Won't you take a seat.

MRS. WARREN. (*Studying him curiously.*) I really can't stay. My name is Karen Warren. My husband and I just moved in next door a week ago.

NORMAN. Hello. My name is Norman Bulansky. Welcome to my seat. Won't you take a home . . . (*Correcting himself.*) A seat. Won't you take my home . . . (*Truly confused.*) Oh boy! This is kind of, you know, oh boy, tricky.

MRS. WARREN. "Welcome to my home. Won't you take a

seat." I think that's it.

NORMAN. No, it can't be that. This is my home, not your home.

MRS. WARREN. I really won't take but a minute.

NORMAN. Won't you take a seat? (*She sits. Barry enters from the bathroom, now strangely energized. He spots Mrs. Warren.*)

BARRY. Hello, My name is Barry Klemper. Welcome to my home. Won't you take a seat?

MRS. WARREN. I'm sitting, thank you.

BARRY. (*With great sociability.*) So you are. How silly of me. (*Sitting beside her.*) Do you enjoy golf?

NORMAN. Can I get you something to drink? We have milk and juice and iced tea and cheese and eggs and . . .

MRS. WARREN. I really have to go. I just dropped by for a second to ask . . .

BARRY. My father's coming for a visit. He'll be in Boston for a few days and he's coming down here for a visit.

MRS. WARREN. That's . . . nice.

NORMAN. Can I give you some iced tea please?

MRS. WARREN. No thank you.

BARRY. Do you know what Dad does? He coaches third base for the New York Yankees. Kipper Klemper is what they call him.

NORMAN. With these keys, I can get into anything.

MRS. WARREN. (*A little desperate.*) I can't stay. I just came by to . . . Well, my little boy, Sean, has two pet hamsters and one of them escaped last night and we thought maybe he might have scurried in here. (*Barry and Norman look to each other. Pause.*)

BARRY. (*With feigned innocence.*) A hamster? Is that in the rat or rabbit family?

NORMAN. Was he big or little?

MRS. WARREN. (*Indicating with her hands.*) Oh, I don't know. Maybe about this big.

NORMAN. Brown or some other color?

BARRY. About the size of two and a half to three golf balls?

MRS. WARREN. Light brown. He was about four inches long and light brown.

BARRY. (*After a beat.*) I haven't see hide nor hair of a hamster. What about you, Norman?

24

NORMAN. I'm Norman Bulansky. Hello. Welcome to my iced tea. (*The apartment goes to black. A darkened movie theatre. Arnold, wearing a maintenance man's uniform, sits in the back row, popcorn in hand. His uniform has the name "Bob" embroidered over a pocket. The lights flicker.*)
ARNOLD. (*To the audience.*) Because I clean up after the matinee, mostly I just see the ends of the movies. Or sometimes the start. But I always seem to miss the story. It's not a bad job. My boss, Mr. Corbin, says I'm doing real good. But frankly, I'm a little worried. On Tuesday, this new usher came. His name is Melvin. And believe me, he looks like a typical Melvin. Big muscles and a thick thick neck. Melvin's got me a little concerned. He says I have to polish his shoes every day or he'll beat me up. He says if I tell anybody, he'll grind me into the pavement. (*He takes shoes from beneath the theatre seat. They are enormous.*) Melvin wears these. They're just black. I'm real glad they're not two-toned or something. (*Back in the apartment. Early evening. A horn honks offstage. Lucien comes out of the bathroom. He wears a robe with his pajamas and slippers. Jack enters.*)
JACK. C'mon, Lucien. Norman and Arnold are already in the van. Aren't you coming?
LUCIEN. I don't wanna be dancing.
JACK. It'll be fun. You always like it when you get there.
LUCIEN. I just had the shower.
JACK. Your hair's not wet.
LUCIEN. I just did my hands and my knees and my feet.
JACK. You're supposed to do your whole body, not just selected parts.
LUCIEN. It's too wet in there.
JACK. Right. So come on. Throw on your dancing clothes and we'll drive over to the Center.
LUCIEN. I got to practice for the State Sneck.
JACK. The State Senate.
LUCIEN. I got a tie with Spiderman. I got to practice. I be showing the Sneck my library card. It's got my name.
JACK. Good idea. (*Horn honks again.*) Now look, throw on some clothes and come to the dance with Norman and Arnold and me.
LUCIEN. No thank you. I got to practice.

25

JACK. Okay. I understand.

LUCIEN. Barry helps Lucien P. Smith. The State Sneck, they read?

JACK. Yeah. They read.

LUCIEN. Oh.

JACK. But they don't care whether you can read or not. They just want you to be yourself. Just answer a few easy questions and be yourself.

LUCIEN. Yourself, it ain't ready yet. Yourself just ain't ready yet. (*Lucien exits slowly into his bedroom. Jack steps forward.*)

JACK. (*To the audience.*) Two nights ago, at around midnight, Lucien pulled a fire alarm. This created quite a flurry of activity. Fires in apartment complexes draw a lot of attention. Lots of equipment. And one particularly enraged fire chief. When he finally tracked Lucien down, Lucien said, "Can I be having some aspirin, please?" When he finally tracked me down, he wasn't in a listening mood. (*A moment.*) When I got home at three A.M., I threw a toaster across the kitchen. Shards of metal all over the place. The next morning, a friend dropped by. "What happened?" he asked. "I'm on a toast-free diet," I said. (*Long pause.*) And we both laughed. (*The dance. A gymnasium floor. Streamers. Balloons. Colored lights. Contemporary popular music. Arnold wears a loud sports jacket, no tie, brown shoes. Norman wears his doughnut shop outfit with a tie. His keys dangle. The men are standing on the periphery, checking things out.*)

ARNOLD. (*Pointing.*) That one! That one. I danced with her two weeks ago. You know what she did? She drooled on me. All over my shoulder. Some of it even got on my pants. I hate that when you dance with a girl and she drools on you. It's very unsanitary. (*Spotting another dancer.*) And that Freddie Golonzo. He thinks he's Xavier Cugat or somebody. Ever since he got those sneakers with the stripes, he thinks he's Xavier Cugat.

NORMAN. Who's Xavier Cugat?

ARNOLD. Just the greatest dancer who ever lived, that's all.

NORMAN. How come your hands are all black?

ARNOLD. Are they? Oh, I been polishing my shoes a lot lately. It's a . . . habit I'm into.

NORMAN. (*Studying Arnold's shoes.*) They look scuffed.

26

ARNOLD. Well, you can't keep them perfect every minute. That'd be an impossibility. Every once in a while, there's going to be scuffs.

NORMAN. I like scuffs.

ARNOLD. (*Again pointing.*) See her! Her name's Helen. She has this wicked tic. Every time she dances, she tics. (*Imitating her tic.*) Like that.

NORMAN. (*Imitating Arnold.*) Like this?

ARNOLD. Sort of. But it's more of a . . . (*He again tics.*) And let me tell you, Norman, a tic like that concerns me.

NORMAN. I know. Who can keep up with it?

ARNOLD. She can't help it. It's a tic. People who got a tic got a tic. They can't do anything about it. It's a behavior pattern. Like a big nose. Or ears that stick out all over the place.

NORMAN. I've seen those kind of cars.

ARNOLD. Frankly, I been watching her tonight and I don't think she's ticked once. Maybe it was just me. Maybe it was just a plan to make me think she had a tic.

NORMAN. (*Imitating the tic.*) It's kind of like this, huh?

ARNOLD. More this way.

NORMAN. That's a pretty bad tic.

ARNOLD. (*Decisively.*) I'm going to cut in. I'm just going to say, "Excuse me, can I cut in?" Jack says we can cut in if we want to.

NORMAN. Go ahead. Cut in.

ARNOLD. "Excuse me, can I cut in?" That's all I'm going to say.

NORMAN. Go ahead.

ARNOLD. I'll be back as soon as this dance is over. (*Arnold exits to the dance floor, a bounce in his step. Norman stands dumbly. Long pause. Finally, Arnold returns.*)

NORMAN. What happened? (*No response.*) Did you cut in? Does she tic or not?

ARNOLD. I figured I'd better wait, you know, for a better time. I gave it some serious consideration and I figured I'd better wait. I don't really feel like dancing anyway. Especially with some girl named Helen who has a tic.

NORMAN. That's maybe better.

ARNOLD. Sure it's better. Just because some stupid girl

named Helen has a tic, she thinks all of a sudden she's the Queen of England. And you know what?

NORMAN. What.

ARNOLD. She's not.

NORMAN. That's maybe better.

ARNOLD. Sure it's better.

NORMAN. That's maybe better.

ARNOLD. Sure it's better. (*The lights switch to Mrs. Fremus and Barry, on her porch, rocking chairs behind them. Night with a moon. Mrs. Fremus has a golf club. Barry, in his golfing attire, studies her awkward swing.*)

MRS. FREMUS. I can't do this anymore. My arthritis is too active.

BARRY. (*Petulantly.*) I borrowed that club just for this lesson.

MRS. FREMUS. I'm sorry, Barry. I just can't. (*She gives Barry the club and returns to her rocker.*)

BARRY. Did I tell you my Dad's coming to visit me?

MRS. FREMUS. That'd be nice. I have the orange rocker in my bedroom. We could sit here.

BARRY. It's a pretty moon tonight. Too bad he couldn't come tonight.

MRS. FREMUS. When we first moved here, Barney said he loved this view more than anything. The way the guard towers stick up over the trees, he loved that. Barney's sister used to say she'd never live anywhere near a prison, but Barney said he'd much prefer to know exactly where the criminal element was.

BARRY. My Dad used to be a backfield coach with the San Francisco Forty-niners. He knew all the guys. All the guys knew him.

MRS. FREMUS. I've got pink lemonade in the freezer. We could sit out here and have lemonade.

BARRY. I haven't seen him in nine years.

MRS. FREMUS. A lot happens in five years, Barry.

BARRY. You know, he's been busy. You know, on the road. But every Christmas, no matter what, he sends me a box of chocolates. Whether he's busy or not. Every Christmas. Oh, a couple of times, you know, the box arrived late, but he never forgets. Not my Dad. (*The lights return to the dance.*

Norman sits silently, gaping at the dancers, playing with his keys. Jack watches for a moment, then comes over.)

JACK. So, what's happening, Norman?

NORMAN. Arnold went to the bathroom and a couple of drips got on his pants, so he won't come out until it dries. He says people are gonna think he pees his pants. "So what?" I said, but he won't come out.

JACK. Yeah. I've had that kind of thing happen to me. It's pretty embarrassing.

NORMAN. Except for that, it's been kinda slow.

JACK. I see you and Sheila aren't dancing. What's the matter?

NORMAN. She's not no Skinny Minnie herself.

JACK. Did you two have a fight? (*Norman nods.*) It's personal. I understand.

NORMAN. I need my keys. I can't get into things without my keys.

JACK. She doesn't like your keys, huh?

NORMAN. She wants my keys!

JACK. (*After a pause.*) She looks pretty sad over there. Why don't you go over and ask her to dance? It'd be a real mature thing to do, Norman.

NORMAN. But, Jack, she wants my keys!

JACK. Just go over there and ask her to dance. Don't even mention the keys. Maybe she's forgotten all about it.

NORMAN. Are you kidding? Oh boy! She's got a memory like a horse.

JACK. All right, I've got another idea. I'll keep the keys with me. Then if she asks about them, you can tell her I'm keeping them for the time being.

NORMAN. No. (*A sudden inspiration.*) Oh boy, I got it!

JACK. You do? What?

NORMAN. I'll ask Sheila to dance. I'm gonna do it now. I'll just . . . ask her. It's a pleasure speaking to you, Jack. I've got to go. (*Norman exits across the dance floor. Jack enjoys him.*)

JACK. (*To the audience.*) Every Wednesday, we have dances here at the Center. Most of the residents come. They drink punch and eat potato chips and pop balloons and hide in the bathroom and, sooner or later, dance. Some of the multiply handicapped just sit on the fringe and watch. It's a curious thing. I've been coming to these dances for months now and I can never decide if it's the saddest place I've ever been. Or the happiest. (*Arnold enters in a somewhat frenetic state. He comes to Jack. The front of his shirt and pants are drenched.*)

ARNOLD. Jack! Oh, am I glad to see you. You won't believe what happened!

JACK. Have you been swimming, Arnold?

ARNOLD. Nope. The faucet in the bathroom went crazy! It exploded! Water all over the place!

JACK. (*Starting to deal with it.*) Great.

ARNOLD. Stop!

JACK. Arnold, I'll be right back . . .

ARNOLD. (*Conspiratorially.*) Don't you get it?

JACK. Get what?

ARNOLD. Oh, this is perfect. Just perfect!

JACK. Okay, Arnold, what's going on?

ARNOLD. Okay, here's what I did. I went to the bathroom and I peed and I was careful as always, but a couple of drops went on my pants. This made me deeply nervous, so I got in one of the stalls and kind of waited for it to, you know, dry. Well, and get this, my pants wouldn't dry! They must be a special chemical or something. They just wouldn't dry! But then I got this great idea. If I was all wet, people wouldn't know it was pee. They'd think it was something else. So I splashed water all over me and, so far, I've told four people that the water on me was an explosion, and not pee. (*A beat.*) I've had great results. (*The lights go to black and come up on a small patio area. Lucien is "planting" tomatoes in a window box, then covering them with dirt. As he does so, he is talking to himself, practicing for the Senate.*)

LUCIEN. (*To the imaginary Senate.*) "Ladies and men of the State Sneck. Lucien P. Smith has Spiderman. I mean business . . . " (*Stops, sings lightly.*) AB . . . CD . . . LMNO . . . Q . . . (*Barry enters. He has the borrowed club.*)

BARRY. I was just with Mrs. Fremus. And in my opinion, she doesn't have the temperment for the pro tour. Under all that pressure, she'd just crumble. She'd get the yips every time she even saw a putter. It's a shame. She's a nice lady. (*Pause.*) Whatcha doing, Lucien?

LUCIEN. I be planting.

30

BARRY. Tomatoes don't grow like that. They come on little . . . bushes.

LUCIEN. We got no bushes. (*Indicating the club.*) Is that golf?

BARRY. It's a five iron. Most useful club in the bag, Lucien. Some men, they sleep with their five irons.

LUCIEN. That must be bumpy.

BARRY. Bumpy or not, it makes for better golf. More serious golf. (*A beat.*) Did I tell you my Dad was coming to visit me?

LUCIEN. That must be bumpy to sleep like that.

BARRY. Did you know that my Dad once played one on one with Bob Cousy and ate him up. Just ate Cousy right up.

LUCIEN. He ate him up?

BARRY. (*On the edge.*) A hook shot here, a driving layup there. Defense! Defense! Defense!

LUCIEN. He ate him up?

BARRY. Lucien, can I tell you something personal? I mean, just between you and me? Roommate to roommate. A secret?

LUCIEN. Norman, he be eating doughnuts all the time.

BARRY. My Dad scares me. He scares me something terrible, Lucien. Something terrible.

LUCIEN. Want some cookies? We got cookies. (*Pause.*) Norman don't eat cookies like he be eating doughnuts.

BARRY. I think I'll go inside and get ready for bed. That's what I think I'll do. I'll go inside and get ready for bed. (*Very disturbed, Barry exits. He leaves the golf club behind. Lucien aware of something amiss, watches silently. Finally he calls to Barry.*)

LUCIEN. Dads, they be scary sometimes. (*Getting no response, Lucien picks up the club and studies it. He again addresses the imaginary Senate.*) "Ladies and men of the Sneck. I am Lucien P. Smith. (*Long pause, finally gets it, delighted.*) Me and Barry golf. Bumpy. Bumpy. Bumpy." (*The lights fade and come up on the dance floor. Norman and Sheila face each other awkwardly. Sheila is an overweight girl in her late twenties, early thirties. She is dressed poorly, speaks poorly. Music plays in the background, as it has throughout most of the dance sequence.*)

NORMAN. Hi, Sheila.

SHEILA. Hi, Norman.

NORMAN. Hi, Sheila.

31

SHEILA. Hi, Norman. (*A long pause, neither of them knowing what to say.*)

NORMAN. Hello, my name is Norman Bulansky. May I hold this dance?

SHEILA. Hi, Norman. (*Norman goes to her and they begin to dance. They are very tentative. They barely move. The music stops abruptly. They look at each other somewhat quizzically. Sheila goes to a bench and sits. Norman follows.*)

NORMAN. It sure was a short song. Oh boy.

SHEILA. The popcorn was good tonight.

NORMAN. I didn't have none.

SHEILA. It was good popcorn. In a bowl. It's nice in a bowl.

NORMAN. I'm on a diet. I just had two handfuls, that's all.

SHEILA. I saw this doughnut today, Norman. At the center.

NORMAN. You saw a doughnut at the Center? Oh boy!

SHEILA. It made me think of you. Mr. Pearl, he ate it up.

NORMAN. I bet it was good. (*The music starts up lightly.*)

SHEILA. Your shirt is nice.

NORMAN. It's my doughnut shop shirt. Jack said I could wear it only once in a while because it's baby.

SHEILA. Your tie is nice.

NORMAN. Barry let me have it. He has lots of ties, so he let me have it.

SHEILA & NORMAN. (*After a beat, together.*) Want to dance? (*A delighted laugh. They again begin to dance.*)

NORMAN. This is a good song. It's got a beat. I wouldn't go to no dance where they didn't have popcorn.

SHEILA. My sister says to dance real good you got to make believe you're a flower.

NORMAN. We got an African violet in the sink.

SHEILA. And you know what flower I'd be?

NORMAN. Oh boy, let me guess. An African violet?

SHEILA. I don't know. But I'd be some kind. (*They continue to dance as Arnold enters and stands facing the audience. His pants and shirt are still drenched. The music softens. Norman and Sheila dance poorly and quietly in the background.*)

ARNOLD. (*To the audience.*) I went up to Helen and she wasn't dancing. She was just sitting there. And I said, "Excuse me, can I cut in?" And she said to me, "You're all wet." Well, that did it. I don't have to take that kind of treatment.

"Oh yeah?" I said. "Well you got a tic!" (*Imitating the tic.*) But, and this is the nub, when we started dancing, she didn't tic at all. (*Pause.*) So what I want to know is, what's she up to? (*Jack enters. He is not amused. He approaches Arnold.*)
JACK. Arnold.
ARNOLD. Hi, Jack. I've fooled three more people. From my point of view, splashing water on your pants is a plan everybody should participate.
JACK. Let's go outside, Arnold.
ARNOLD. Sure, Jack. But I repeat, I could catch a draft and have to take antibiotics. (*Jack moves "outside." Arnold follows.*)
JACK. Arnold, what did you tell Helen?
ARNOLD. Nothing. Nothing much. Just chitchat.
JACK. What did you tell her?
ARNOLD. I told her she had a tic. (*Imitating tic.*) Like this.
JACK. You can't go around insulting people, Arnold. You upset Helen. She's in the van now and she won't talk and she won't come out.
ARNOLD. She started it. She said, and I mean this frankly, Jack, that I was all wet.
JACK. You are all wet.
ARNOLD. Oh, yeah!
JACK. Yeah!
ARNOLD. (*With anger.*) Well, you got a tic!!
JACK. (*Frustrated, to himself.*) Jesus . . .
ARNOLD. And don't swear, Jack. It's not polite.
JACK. (*Exploding.*) Don't tell me what to do, Arnold! Okay! Don't tell me what to do, goddamn it! I've had it with all of you telling me what to do! I've had it with the whole god-damn bunch of you!!! Christ!!! (*Arnold is stunned. And hurt. He starts back inside, then turns on Jack.*)
ARNOLD. You've got behavior patterns that are not fun, Jack! Not, I repeat, one bit fun! (*Arnold exits. Jack stands emptily.*)
JACK. (*To the audience.*) Every time I lose my temper with these guys, I hate myself for about a week. (*Pause.*) I need a new job. They deserve better. Or I deserve better. Or some-body deserves something. (*Jack walks away. The music stops. Norman and Sheila end their dance.*)

SHEILA. *(Applauding lightly.)* That was nice.

NORMAN. *(Copying her applause.)* Oh boy. That was nice.

SHEILA. Norman?

NORMAN. Yeah?

SHEILA. Can I have your keys?

NORMAN. I need my keys.

SHEILA. Please, Norman.

NORMAN. I need my keys. I can't get into things without my keys.

SHEILA. Can I have them?

NORMAN. *(With finality.)* I need my keys, Sheila! I need my keys! *(Pause. They both pout as the music starts up lightly.)*

SHEILA. I like the slow parts.

NORMAN. Me too. I like songs with a beat. *(They begin to dance.)*

SHEILA. Guess what, Norman? I'm a geranium.

NORMAN. Not me.

SHEILA. *(After a step or two.)* Norman, what flower are you?

NORMAN. An apple doughnut with raisins.

SHEILA. That's nice. I'm a geranium. *(They dance. And from their shuffling awkward step, Norman and Sheila are transformed. The lights intensify. The music builds. They glide effortlessly across the floor, no longer Norman and Sheila, but something else. Ginger Rogers and Fred Astaire. The King and Queen of the prom. They move beautifully, confidently, and there is no vestige of their real selves.)*

FADE to BLACKOUT.

END OF ACT I.

ACT II

Still summer. The library. Lucien walks with a pile of ominous tomes. Above him hangs a large nineteenth century portrait of a past benefactor. Lucien spots the portrait and stops. He places the books down, and approaches the painting. He gets a chair. He stands on the chair and studies the portrait face-to-face. He surveys the room. He imitates the arms-crossed pose of the portrait. He is pleased.

LUCIEN. (*To the imaginary Senate.*) "Ladies and men of the State Sneck. I be Lucien P. Smith and I mean business." (*Stops, looks down.*) This be high. (*His speech again.*) "Ladies and men of the Sneck . . . This be high." (*Waving, a great smile.*) Hi! (*Laughs, enjoying himself, now waving graciously to an imaginary crowd.*) Hi, everybody being everywhere, hi! Lucien P. Smith says, "Hi! Have a nice day! Hi!!!" (*The lights fade and come up on the back of the movie theatre. Arnold, in his maintenance uniform, is polishing a pair of two-toned dress shoes.*)
ARNOLD. (*To the audience.*) Melvin gave me these to do. He's got to go to a wedding. He said if I didn't do a good job, he was gonna turn me into pulp. That really got me. "Oh yeah," I said. "What's pulp?" (*Brushes more, then looks up.*) I had my first run-in with Mr. Corbin last week. He's the movie manager. He's a nice guy, but frankly, the bathrooms, and I mean this honestly, aren't too important to him. And here's how I know. I asked him to look at the number three urinal. It seemed to be going down slow. You know what he said? He said, "Arnold, that's your problem." I couldn't believe it. What does he think I am? An architect? (*Morning in the apartment. Norman is in the kitchen doing dishes. He wears an apron and his doughnut shop shirt. Lucien is vacuuming. The cord, however, is still wrapped on the machine and not plugged in. Norman watches for a moment.*)
NORMAN. You got to turn it on.
LUCIEN. It's hard.
NORMAN. You got to plug in the plug, Lucien.
LUCIEN. I forgot.

35

NORMAN. If you don't turn it on, it won't pick up nothing.

LUCIEN. I forgot.

NORMAN. I saw Sheila yesterday at the Center. She's pretty nice.

LUCIEN. When you plug it, it be loud.

NORMAN. We're gonna have one baby boy and one baby girl. And every day, they'll all come with me to the doughnut shop. And you know what? Free doughnuts.

LUCIEN. (*Dusting ineffectually.*) Norman, where do dust come from?

NORMAN. From trees.

LUCIEN. Oh.

NORMAN. And when the baby boy and the baby girl get real big, Sheila and me, oh boy, we'll give them crullers. Free.

LUCIEN. We got no trees. (*The doorbell rings.*)

NORMAN. Come in! My name is Norman Bulansky! Welcome to my home!

LUCIEN. (*Also shouting to the door.*) We got no trees! (*Jack enters, nursing a cut finger.*)

JACK. Good morning, guys. What's happening?

NORMAN. Hi, Jack. How are you? The job's going great. Nice to see you again. What happened to your finger?

JACK. Oh, I just cut it in the car.

NORMAN. You want to lie down?

JACK. It's nothing, Norman. Just a little scrape. (*Lucien goes to Jack and wraps the dirty rag gently around his cut hand.*)

JACK. What are you doing, Lucien?

LUCIEN. It'll fix it better.

JACK. (*Touched.*) Thanks, Lucien. It feels better already.

NORMAN. That's got all dust on it.

JACK. It's a tourniquet, Norman. Just to stop the bleeding. I'll clean it in a second.

LUCIEN. (*Goes to the door and yells out.*) We got no trees!

JACK. That's telling 'em, Lucien. So where are the other two Musketeers?

NORMAN. Arnold's out beating the rugs, but Barry, he says he won't help. He's too busy.

JACK. Arnold's out beating what rugs?

NORMAN. The rugs.

JACK. Oh, those rugs. And Barry won't help?

NORMAN. He's right down on the list to clean the bathroom, but he says 'cause his Dad's coming to visit, he ain't got no time. And you know what? He's golfing. I saw him out in front. He's golfing.

LUCIEN. (*Inspecting Jack's other hand.*) This one's good.

JACK. I didn't cut that one. I cut the other one.

NORMAN. He says 'cause his Dad's coming to visit he needs to get ready so he says he don't have to clean nothing.

JACK. I'll talk to him, Norman. He's under a lot of pressure, a lot of strain.

LUCIEN. Just tell me to, and I'll be going to the hospital.

JACK. I think I'll just go wash it off and put a Band-Aid on it.

NORMAN. If my Dad came, I'd still do the dishes.

JACK. I thought your father was dead, Norman.

NORMAN. So what? Oh boy, so what! Just because he's dead doesn't mean I wouldn't do the dishes. I'd still do the dishes. Just because a guy is dead doesn't mean people won't do dishes!

JACK. You're right, Norman. I lost my head. I'll be right back. (*Jack exits into the bathroom.*)

LUCIEN. My Daddy, he be dead too.

NORMAN. Would you do the dishes?

LUCIEN. No thank you. I be dusting. (*Arnold enters in his usual frenzy. He carries a small bath mat and an equally small welcome mat.*)

ARNOLD. Where's Jack? I saw his car. I've got to have a talk with him. This is very important.

LUCIEN. In the bathroom.

ARNOLD. This can't wait. This is crucial. (*Calling in to the bathroom.*) Excuse me, Jack, but we have to have a discussion!

JACK. (*Off, in the bathroom.*) I'll be right out, Arnold. Hold your horses.

ARNOLD. Hold my horses?

LUCIEN. You got horses?

ARNOLD. He must have me confused with someone else. I don't have any horses. (*Calling into the bathroom.*) It's me Arnold!

LUCIEN. (*Yelling to the door.*) We got no trees! (*Jack enters from the bathroom, a Band-Aid on his finger.*)

JACK. Okay, Arnold, what's the big emergency?

ARNOLD. How are you, Jack? It's nice to see you.

JACK. And a pleasure to see you. What's the emergency?

ARNOLD. The rugs.

JACK. Of course.

ARNOLD. I had a little problem with the rugs.

JACK. What rugs?

ARNOLD. (*Holding up the mats.*) These rugs.

LUCIEN. You got horses, Arnold?

ARNOLD. He's doing it again, Jack. I told you this bothers me. First it was bunnies, now it's horses. It's a behavior pattern.

NORMAN. (*Still struggling with the dishes.*) We got to make it illegal to have lemonade. It won't come out. I scrub and scrub and it won't come out.

LUCIEN. Who's got a bunny?

ARNOLD. You see, there! He did it again. I do not, I repeat, have a bunny. I do not, I repeat, I do not, I repeat, have a bunny.

JACK. Okay, Arnold, let's drift our way back to the rugs.

ARNOLD. He's got me so worried with this bunny, I can hardly think.

JACK. Lucien, please stop talking about bunnies.

ARNOLD. And no more cheese. Cheese sticks.

NORMAN. If we can't have cheese, I'll go on a hunger strike. (*Barry enters by the front door. He wears his golf outfit. He carries a blank cardboard sign and a box of crayons. He goes straight for his bedroom.*)

LUCIEN. Hi, Barry.

BARRY. Hi, Lucien. Jack.

JACK. Barry.

BARRY. Arnold. Norman.

NORMAN. I don't talk to people who don't do dishes. That's a law I made up. I don't care if anybody's dead or what.

BARRY. If you people will excuse me, I have business. Mrs. Fremus let me borrow these crayons. They belonged to her husband. He was very artistic. He was in the roofing tile game. (*Barry exits into his bedroom.*)

NORMAN. Just because he golfs, he thinks he's Xavier Cugat or somebody.

JACK. So, Arnold, when last we tuned in to the planet Xenon, there was something about rugs.

ARNOLD. I almost forgot. The rugs. I forgot about the rugs. Thanks for reminding me. This is important.

NORMAN. And eggs. I'm sick of eggs. Eggs stick.

ARNOLD. Does anybody care about the rugs, or what?

LUCIEN. Eggs come out of chickens.

ARNOLD. Does anybody care about the rugs or is it just me? Because if it's just me, I'm not telling. Take it or leave it.

NORMAN. Sometimes the suds get so big you can't see nothing in the sink.

LUCIEN. Let me see.

NORMAN. It's very weird, huh?

LUCIEN. (*Putting his face in the suds-filled sink.*) You can't see nothing.

ARNOLD. Okay. Fine. Nobody cares about the rugs. Fine. If anybody wants me, I'll be in my room thinking about the rugs. And if somebody, for example, wants to know what happened with the rugs, they'll have to get me to tell them. And frankly, I'm not telling anybody anyway, so anyone who asks is just in for a big surprise. (*He starts for his room, stops.*)

NORMAN. Oh boy, Lucien, oh boy!

ARNOLD. When I move to Russia, if they give me a roommate who says "Oh boy" all the time, I as an American citizen will say *nyet* to that. *Nyet, nyet, nyet.*

NORMAN. Oh boy, what's "*nyet*"? Oh boy, *nyet.* What's "*nyet*"?

ARNOLD. (*Gets the rugs.*) I think I'll be needing these. Call it a behavior pattern if you want, but that's the way I see it. (*Arnold exits into his bedroom.*)

NORMAN. (*Firmly, tossing his apron aside.*) I quit!

JACK. You can't quit, Norman. You have to finish your chores. But you can take a break. Go on. Take a break.

NORMAN. (*Just as firmly.*) I'm taking a break!

LUCIEN. (*To Arnold's closed door.*) You be thinking about the rugs?

ARNOLD. (*Off, in his bedroom.*) Loose lips sink ships!

BARRY. (*Off, in his bedroom.*) Keep it down out there! I'm doing merchandising!

ARNOLD. (*Off.*) Loose lips sink ships!

LUCIEN. (*To nobody in particular.*) We got no trees! (*Silence. Lucien gets another rag and dusts. Norman sidles up to Jack.*)

NORMAN. Jack?

JACK. Yeah?

NORMAN. Can Sheila come here some time? Just me and her alone? I'd like her to see my . . . pad.

JACK. That's a tricky one, Norman. I'll have to think about it.

NORMAN. Please, Jack.

JACK. I'll see what I can do.

NORMAN. It's my pad. I'd like her to see it. Barry says if you call it a pad, girls will come over because . . . I'm not sure.

JACK. You'll probably attract a lot of beatniks.

NORMAN. I don't care, but they have to bring their own doughnuts. (*Barry emerges from his room. He has a hand-lettered sign.*)

BARRY. I'm done. What do you guys think?

JACK. (*Reading the sign.*) "Price War! Learn Golf. 2 Lessons for 25 cents." That's great, Barry.

BARRY. It's a merchandising technique. "Price War!" That excites the average person.

LUCIEN. (*Giving Barry a penny.*) Okay. Lucien P. Smith wants to.

BARRY. What's this?

LUCIEN. Money.

BARRY. This is a penny. Lessons are twenty-five cents, Lucien.

NORMAN. I don't talk to people who don't do dishes.

BARRY. Jack, would you please explain some of the realities to Lucien. Realities like how I can't run a business on a penny here and a penny there. Would you please explain that to him? I haven't got the patience.

JACK. Sure. Lucien, Barry can't run a business on a penny here and a penny there.

BARRY. Be sarcastic, Jack. That helps. Sure. That helps the situation. Sure.

ARNOLD. (*Popping his head into the room.*) I repeat, I am in here, I repeat, thinking about the rugs!

LUCIEN. (*Giving Barry another penny.*) Here's more.

ARNOLD. (*Off.*) Loose lips sink ships!

BARRY. Another penny. Is this a joke? Is golf suddenly a big joke?

JACK. He wants more money, Lucien. Twenty-three more cents.

LUCIEN. I be getting it. (*Lucien exits purposefully into his bedroom.*)

NORMAN. I don't like golf.

BARRY. Golf is a way of life, Norman. It's not for everybody. Fat people shouldn't golf anyway.

NORMAN. Fat? Oh boy! Look who's calling who fat? Oh boy!

BARRY. Fat guys can't even reach down and get the ball out of the cup. Fat guys need caddies everywhere they go.

NORMAN. Oh boy! Fat! Oh boy!

JACK. Fellas . . .

NORMAN. Look who's calling who fat? Oh boy!

JACK. That's enough. (*Arnold enters from his bedroom. He has the rugs. He heads for the front door with determination.*)

ARNOLD. I'm going to be fair about this. I've thought about it, and I've decided to be fair. So here's what I'm gonna do. I'm going outside to where the whole rug thing happened, and I'm going to tell the whole story out loud to whoever is interested enough to listen. And all I can say is, you can (A) take it, or (B) leave it. (*No reaction.*) Frankly, in Russia, rugs are more important than golf! (*Arnold exits by the front door.*)

BARRY. He took the welcome mat. Did you see that, Jack? Arnold took the welcome mat.

NORMAN. Oh boy, now nobody'll come to visit.

JACK. He's bringing it right back. (*Arnold pops in the door. He has been listening outside.*)

ARNOLD. No, I'm not!

NORMAN. He's back pretty fast.

ARNOLD. Norman, I've been thinking about this and you're the only guy I'm going to tell. Follow me.

41

NORMAN. I got to do dishes.

BARRY. The last time you did dishes, there was cheese all over the plates.

NORMAN. Cheese? Oh boy, cheese. Did he say cheese?

JACK. Okay, guys, why don't we take a rest?

ARNOLD. Are you coming or not? These rugs are giving me muscle cramps.

BARRY. You should have your eyesight checked.

NORMAN. Oh boy, did he say I was fat? Did he? Just tell me.

JACK. He said you should get your eyesight checked.

NORMAN. Oh yeah?

ARNOLD. I'm leaving. I'm not going to waste the best part of the day just standing here, I emphasize, chitchatting. (*Arnold exits out the front door.*)

BARRY. You should get a Seeing Eye dog when you do dishes.

JACK. Cool it, Barry. That's enough of that stuff.

NORMAN. Golf sups!

BARRY. What?

NORMAN. Golf sups! And I don't care if anybody hears me. It sups! It sups! Golf sups!!! (*Norman exits triumphantly.*)

BARRY. (*Calling after him.*) Golf sucks! It doesn't sup! It sucks! Golf sucks! (*Pause, agitated.*) If I had lots of money, I'd go to Florida now. Really. I'd go down there, play a few rounds every day, lie on the beach and listen to the radio, maybe even bring a thermos full of highballs. Maybe even take my Dad. Yeah, I'd take Dad. (*Pause.*) Today is Saturday. In just two days, he'll be here. Of course, he'll probably look older. People look older. That's just the aging process.

JACK. Nine years is a long time.

BARRY. (*Starkly.*) My Dad, you know, when Mom died, he was pretty busy with his career. So when he brought me out to the Institutions, he couldn't stay around too long. He kind of waved. (*Barry cannot continue. He is very disturbed. Pause.*)

JACK. Why don't we take a walk?

BARRY. No. You go. I want to stay here.

JACK. Are you sure? You know, I go out golfing once in a while. I'm not very good. I could probably use a pointer or two.

BARRY. You're just being nice, Jack.

JACK. I'll tell you what. Maybe I'll take a walk, then, in ten minutes or so, I'll come back. I'll go listen to Arnold talk about the rugs.

BARRY. You tell him I want that welcome mat back here before my Dad comes. You tell him that, okay?

JACK. Sure.

BARRY. I could use the time, you know, the time alone.

JACK. Sure. I'll be right back. (*Jack quietly exits. Barry sits motionlessly. Lucien enters from his bedroom. He carries a handful of buttons.*)

LUCIEN. Hey, Barry, I got this for golf.

BARRY. Those are buttons, Lucien. That isn't money. Those are buttons.

LUCIEN. It's all I could be finding. They be good for golf?

BARRY. Every Christmas, no matter what, those chocolates came.

LUCIEN. Buttons are good, Barry. They are.

BARRY. But, and I guess Dad just forgot this, but I never really liked chocolate very much. I'd get stomachaches from it, you know. So I gave it to all the other guys on the ward. Every Christmas. We had this one guy named Wally something, who'd eat the chocolate part and save all the insides in a box he had. And he'd keep the box with him all the time. Until one day he died and one of the attendants just threw the box away. I mean, it was all Wally owned, this box of the insides of all the chocolates he'd ever had, and they just threw it away. They didn't even ask his family or anything. I don't understand that. They didn't even look to see inside. They just threw it away. (*Barry breaks down and sobs. Lucien studies him. Finally, Lucien goes to him and pats his head gently. Over and over. The lights in the apartment fade and come up on the dance floor. Jack is dealing with some party decorations.*)

JACK. (*To the audience.*) I used to have an uncle, Uncle Roland, who said, "Sex is dirty. Money is evil. And death keeps it all in perspective." (*Pause.*) About death: the residents don't think much about death. Either you got it or you don't. And if you do, wait a while, it'll go away. (*Pause.*) About money: Lucien and Barry do assembly work at the sheltered workshop at the Center. The pay is minimal, but since most of their expenses are taken care of, they somehow accumulate money. Both Norman and Arnold do even better from their outside jobs. Last week, Norman wanted a hair dryer. I said it was okay. He gave it away at work as a door prize to the customer who ordered the most doughnuts. Norman sang a few bars of "Happy Birthday." (*Pause.*) And about sex: the official policy is that sex between residents is to be discouraged. It leads to personal crises and legal entanglements. The unofficial view is more liberal. Many of the women have been sterilized, and those who might be sexually active are given birth control pills. Pregnancy, for obvious reasons, is a potential disaster. But what amazes me is this: In a society where inexplicable lusts are rampant and expected, why is it that sexual desire among the mentally deficient is viewed as an additional aberration? My last job interview, my fourteenth in two months, ended with a pigeon-like woman saying I was overqualified and overeducated. "And oversexed," I added with a smile. She didn't smile back. (*Pause.*) Uncle Roland also used to say, "The quickest way to a man's crotch is through his crotch." Yes, Uncle Roland was quite a lightweight. (*Jack exits. Music and lights. Sheila sits on a bench. Clara sits next to her. Clara, clearly very retarded, guards a bowl of popcorn and eats furtively. When she speaks, it is almost a growl.*)

SHEILA. (*The conspirator.*) Clara, there's Norman! See him. He's the big one. Arnold is the other one. Don't talk to Arnold. All he wants to do is talk. Oh, here he comes! He's a big one, isn't he? (*Norman enters. He wears his doughnut shop shirt, his keys, a tie, the works. He stands facing Sheila. Long pause.*) Hi, Norman.

NORMAN. Hi, Sheila.

SHEILA. Hi, Norman.

NORMAN. Hi, Sheila. My name is Norman Bulansky. Welcome to my dance. Won't you take a seat?

SHEILA. This is Clara.

NORMAN. Hi, Clara. My name is Norman Bulansky. Welcome to my home. Won't you take a seat? Can I have your popcorn?

CLARA. No!

SHEILA. She don't say much.

NORMAN. Arnold says he don't know if Helen has a tic or not. Oh boy! So he asked her to dance.
CLARA. Nnnoooo. (*Pause. Norman sits down. Clara and her popcorn are between Norman and Sheila on the bench.*)
NORMAN. It's a good dance tonight, isn't it?
SHEILA. This is Clara. She's a new girl.
NORMAN. At the doughnut shop we got a new girl. She has sort of a mustache. (*To Clara.*) Do you know her?
SHEILA. Girls don't have mustaches.
NORMAN. This one does. One of the girls said the only way to get rid of it is with putting her whole face in electricity.
SHEILA. Ick! Oh no, ick!
CLARA. (*In a low chant.*) No no no no no no no no no no no no no no no no no no no . . . (*Pause. Norman summons his courage.*)
NORMAN. Sheila, want to see my pad?
CLARA. No.
SHEILA. He asked me, Clara. You shut up. What's a pad?
NORMAN. It'd be maybe better if I moved over. (*Norman gets up and tries to squeeze between Sheila and Clara.*)
CLARA. (*With ferocity.*) No!!!
NORMAN. (*Backs off.*) I just thought it'd maybe be better. Oh boy, this is tricky. I'll just sit back down. (*Sits.*) It's okay, Sheila. I can hear you over here. My ears are like cats. (*Pause.*) Sheila, want to see my pad?
CLARA. (*Together with Sheila.*) No!
SHEILA. (*Together with Clara.*) Yes!
NORMAN. It's real nice. We got this big curtain in the bathroom with swans all over it. And we got a couch. And, oh boy, you should just see how we got chairs and pictures and dishes and milk and just about everything. We got lamps. We got doughnuts. And swans. And iced tea. And we got lamps. And want to? Want to see my pad?
CLARA. (*Together with Sheila.*) No!
SHEILA. (*Together with Clara.*) Yes! (*Long pause. Norman quietly glows. Clara eats.*)
SHEILA. Norman?
NORMAN. Yeah?
SHEILA. Can I have your keys?

45

NORMAN. I need my keys.

SHEILA. Please, can I have them?

NORMAN. (*In utter frustration.*) I need my keys, Sheila. I need my keys. I can't get into things without my keys. I need my keys!!!

CLARA. Nonononononononononononononono. . . .

(*The dance floor goes to black. The theatre manager's office. Mr. Corbin is a mild mannered middle-aged man. He is busy dealing with some papers. Arnold, in his maintenance uniform, enters. He carries a handful of sanitary napkins. He is outraged.*)

ARNOLD. Mr. Corbin?

MR. CORBIN. Hi, Arnold. How's it going?

ARNOLD. Hello, Mr. Corbin. It's nice to see you again. But, to be frank about this, I don't have time for chitchat.

MR. CORBIN. All right, Arnold, I can appreciate that. What's on your mind?

ARNOLD. These!

MR. CORBIN. These?

ARNOLD. I have had it with these! Had it! Had it! Had it!

MR. CORBIN. These are sanitary napkins, Arnold.

ARNOLD. I don't care what they are. It isn't fair and I have had it! If I don't have to fill them up in the men's room, I'm not filling them up in the ladies' room! I'm sorry, but end of subject!

MR. CORBIN. Arnold, men and women have different needs.

ARNOLD. Okeydokey! Okeydokey! (*Arnold starts to leave, turns back.*) Frankly, Mr. Corbin, one other thing. I repeat. (*Indicating "Bob" on his uniform.*) Who is "Bob"? (*Arnold turns on his heel and exits. Mr. Corbin, now holding the sanitary napkins, laughs. Back in the apartment. Barry is finishing taping a large cardboard sign over the bathroom door. It reads, "Welcome Home, Dad!" Barry is wearing a dashing new golf outfit. He steps back from the sign. He is not sure. He is very on edge. The doorbell rings. Barry is unsure of what to do. He exits quickly into his bedroom. He emerges immediately with new golf shoes. The doorbell rings again. Barry looks around, then goes to the couch. He sits frozen. The front door opens. Jack enters cautiously, leaving the door open behind him.*)

JACK. Barry?

BARRY. Is he here?

JACK. Yeah. He . . . he just wanted a minute alone. He's pretty nervous.

BARRY. Me too.

JACK. You look great.

BARRY. I got these shoes special. Special for this, you know. A guy wearing shoes like these is almost guaranteed to pick up twenty, thirty yards on the long irons. (*A moment.*) Did Dad tell you about how he and Ted Williams used to go fishing together?

JACK. (*Uncomfortably.*) No. No, he didn't.

BARRY. They caught some beauties. Kipper Klemper and the Splendid Splinter. They were quite a combination.

JACK. Barry, don't be too nervous, okay? He's your father. He cares about you, okay?

BARRY. I had this fight with Arnold this morning. He wouldn't tell me where he hid the welcome mat. "Loose lips sink ships," was all he'd say.

MR. KLEMPER. (*Off, in the hallway.*) Where the hell is it? Is this it? Jack!

JACK. Right in here, Mr. Klemper.

MR. KLEMPER. (*Off.*) My bladder's just about to pop wide open!

JACK. In here! (*To Barry.*) Okay? (*Barry is frozen. Mr. Klemper enters. He is a coarse middle-aged man. He is dressed poorly. He needs a shave. He carries a crumpled paper bag. He has one arm.*)

MR. KLEMPER. These goddamn apartment zoos are all like a maze. Built for goddamn rats. Wouldn't live in one of these sties for all the tea in goddamn China. (*Seeing Barry, stopped cold.*) So this is my little Barry. Grown up real good. Real good. A . . . real man. Real good. (*Pause.*) Where's the pisser in this dump anyhow?

JACK. (*Indicating the bathroom.*) Right there.

MR. KLEMPER. (*Tossing the bag in Barry's lap.*) Got you this. It's just a little something. Be right out. (*Sees the sign.*) You do this, Barry? It's real nice. "Welcome, Home, Dad!" Real thoughtful. (*He carelessly removes it from the door.*) If it's piss or sentiment, give me piss every time. (*Mr. Klemper exits into the bathroom.*)

JACK. What do you think's in the bag?

BARRY. Huh?

JACK. When he comes out, why don't you say hello?

BARRY. Sure, Jack. Sure. Of course.

JACK. He got you a present.

BARRY. I thought I'd wait to open it until he was done. I figure that's the proper way. It's polite that way, you know what I mean?

JACK. Sure.

BARRY. Some people don't have manners. But I'm not one of them. Not on the tour. I'd say golf etiquette, a thorough working knowledge of golf etiquette, is more important to your scratch player than a seven iron. I really mean that.

JACK. I'm sure.

BARRY. Etiquette is birdie country. (*Mr. Klemper enters from the bathroom. Looks around.*)

MR. KLEMPER. It's a nice place you got here, Barry. A real nice homey feeling to it. It seems to be real convenient to shopping and the bars. Of course, me, I couldn't ever relax living so close to a prison. (*Laughing self-consciously.*) So, why don't you open it up? (*No response.*) What's the story here, Jack? Can't he talk?

JACK. He can talk.

BARRY. Hello. My name is Barry Klemper. Welcome to my home. Won't you take a seat?

MR. KLEMPER. I think I'll stand. Those buses put the seats so close together it's a goddamn wonder I don't have a hernia. But thanks for the offer.

JACK. Why don't you see what's in the bag, Barry?

MR. KLEMPER. It's nothing. Just a little something. Nothing. (*Barry reaches in the bag and pulls out a cheap boxed heart. The heart is visible through cellophane. It is broken.*)

JACK. (*Embarrassed.*) A chocolate heart. That's great, Mr. Klemper.

BARRY. (*By rote.*) Thank you very much. I appreciate it. Thank you.

MR. KLEMPER. Like I said, it's just a thought. You can take that cellophane off if you want to. They just put it on to keep it fresh.

BARRY. Thank you very much. I appreciate it. Thank you.

MR. KLEMPER. (*Nervous loud stream of consciousness.*) My

scheme was to get you a box, you know, like always. A nice box of Fanny Farmer, something like that. One of those boxes where inside they got a cherry wrapped up fancy in tinfoil. But I was kind of in a rush, so I had to pick it up at the bus station. They got a gift shop at the bus station. Gifts, cigarettes, gum. Anyway, they didn't have any chocolates. I asked. But then the lady said they had this. This chocolate heart. Well, right away I could see that the goddamn thing was all broken into pieces. "It's damaged," I told the lady. "It's been here since Valentine's Day," she said. "The goddamn thing is damaged," I told her. They get sassy with me, I get sassy right back. They think, a one-armed man, he won't be sassy. Well, bullshit to that. So I said to her, "I'll give you half price." And get this? The old sow said yes. (*Silence. Barry is still. Mr. Klemper paces uncomfortably. Jack is simply embarrassed.*) You know, Jack, maybe the boy'd loosen up if we had a few minutes just the two of us alone. Would you mind?
JACK. (*With reservation.*) Sure. I'll take a little walk. Is that okay with you, Barry?
BARRY. Huh?
JACK. I'll be right back. Okay?
BARRY. Sure, Jack. Okay. Sure. (*Jack takes a moment. Mr. Klemper looks away. Barry is frozen. Jack exits.*)
MR. KLEMPER. Yeah, it's real nice here, Barry. A nice setup. I heard your roommate was a darkie. (*Pause.*) So what have you been doing with yourself?
BARRY. Won't you take a seat?

MR. KLEMPER. I'll stand. (*Long pause.*) So what have you got to say for yourself, boy? (*Silence. Mr. Klemper is getting progressively more frustrated.*) Your mother, God rest her pathetic soul, used to worry that you'd never talk. It wasn't until you were about three that you said your first word. You know what that word was? "Bitch." Your mother and me, we thought that was about the funniest thing we ever heard. We took you right over to Auntie Mae's house so she could hear it. And you said it again, "Bitch." Clear as a bell. We were real proud of you, boy. Real proud. "Bitch." I'll never forget it. (*Stops.*) Are you going to talk, boy, or are you going to keep it up with this silent crap? (*No response.*) I'm talking to you, you little

49

sonovabitch! I'm your goddamn father. When your goddamn father talks, you better goddamn listen. (*Nothing.*) You
hear me boy? This is your father, not some goddamn darkie
roommate. This is your father! You hear me boy? You goddamn nut!! (*Mr. Klemper, impulsively, violently, slaps Barry
across the side of the head. Barry recoils, then instinctively draws
into a fetal position on the couch. Mr. Klemper backs off, shocked by
his own violence. Barry protects himself and moans.*)
BARRY. No, Dad! No more, Dad. Please, Dad. No
more . . . Don't hit me anymore! Please, Dad . . .
MR. KLEMPER. No, no I'm sorry. I . . . lost control.
Jesus, Barry, I didn't mean to . . . I'm sorry, I . . .
BARRY. (*Whimpering.*) No, Dad. Please, Dad. Don't hit
me . . . Please . . .
MR. KLEMPER. (*Paralyzed.*) It was . . . It was an accident,
Barry. I didn't mean to. I just . . . you know . . . lost
control. I'm sorry. Jesus . . . (*Barry stops whimpering. War-
ily, he rights himself. There is nothing for either of them to say. Mr.
Klemper starts for the door.*)
MR. KLEMPER. Well, I . . . I guess I'd better go. Those
buses, they run right on time. Buses don't wait for a one-
armed man. That's one thing I've learned in life, Barry.
Buses don't wait for a one-armed man. (*Pause.*) And don't
you worry, boy. Christmas comes around, those chocolates
will be in the mail. Count on it. (*Pause.*) It ain't my way,
Barry, but your mother, God rest her pathetic soul, would
want you to know that when you were just a little baby who
couldn't talk or nothing, she loved you more than life itself.
More than goddamned life itself. (*Mr. Klemper exits. Barry
calls weakly to the closed door.*)
BARRY. Dad. Dad, I'm a golf pro now, Dad. (*Barry places the
chocolates beside him gently, his mind millions of miles away.
Fade to blackout. The light come up on Arnold at the movie theatre.
He is polishing a pair of huge cowboy boots. He looks up.*)
ARNOLD. (*To the audience.*) These are Melvin's. Personally, I
as a person would never wear cowboy boots. I'm what you call a
landlubber. Not Melvin though. He even said one day if he had
the money, he'd buy a horse. Not me, no sir. Do you have any
idea what horses eat? I don't. (*Pause.*) And frankly, I repeat, I

emphasize, this whole Melvin thing has given me such bags under my eyes, you'd think I had amnesia. *(The lights go to black. Taped Introduction into the State Senate.)*
ANNOUNCEMENT. *(Off.)* Room 313. Health and Human Services Subcommittee. Senator Warren Clarke presiding. Order please. *(The State Senate Chambers. Lucien and Jack sit at a table. Both men wear suits. Lucien has his Spiderman tie. Facing them sits Senator Clarke. Clarke is a dignified middle-aged man. Lucien, very nervous, can barely look up.)*
CLARKE. Mr. Smith, we're very happy you were able to join us today. As our staff has informed you, this subcommittee is only interested in the truth. Therefore, there are no right or wrong answers. Do you understand that, Mr. Smith?
LUCIEN. *(Mumbling.)* I got Spiderman . . .
CLARKE. Mr. Smith, we didn't hear that. You'll have to speak a bit louder.
LUCIEN. *(Quickly standing and showing the tie to the whole room.)* I got Spiderman. Lucien P. Smith, I got Spiderman! I mean business.
CLARKE. *(Embarrassed.)* A Spiderman tie. That's very nice.
LUCIEN. Lucien P. Smith, I mean business.
JACK. *(Guiding Lucien back down.)* They know, Lucien. They know.
CLARKE. *(Awkwardly, gently.)* Mr. Smith . . . uh . . . I'll tell you what, why don't you tell us a little about where you live, your home. Could you do that for us, Mr. Smith?
LUCIEN. *(Singing proudly.)* A B C D L M N O P . . . *(Stops, disoriented, starts again.)* A B L M N O . . . It's hard. You know, it's hard . . . *(Silence in the chambers. Clarke, touched, starts again.)*
CLARKE. That was very nice, Lucien. Please, why don't you tell us about your friends.
LUCIEN. Okay, Jack? We done?
JACK. Not yet, Lucien. Go on, tell the people about home. About Arnold and Norman and . . . Barry. Just tell them what it's like.
LUCIEN. *(After a moment.)* Norman, he be the doughnut man.
CLARKE. The doughnut man? Why do you call him that?
LUCIEN. He be fat with doughnuts. Arnold's got the rugs.

51

He's like nuts or something. He's my friend too. And Barry. He golfs. He be gone now. I miss Barry. I do. I miss Barry. *(Pause, sings again.)* A B C D E F . . . *(Silence. Lucien buries his head in his hands. He cannot continue. Clarke only watches. Slowly the lights change until Clarke and Jack are in darkness and Lucien is in full focus. He looks up. He stands. He is no longer the retarded Lucien, but rather a confident and articulate man. He takes the floor. To the audience, the Senate.)* I stand before you, a middle-aged man in an uncomfortable suit, a man whose capacity for rational thought is somewhere between a five-year-old and an oyster. *(Pause.)* I am retarded. I am damaged. I am sick inside from so many years of confusion, utter and profound confusion. I am mystified by faucets and radios and elevators and newspapers and popular songs. I cannot always remember the names of my parents. But I will not go away. And I will not wither because the cage is too small. I am here to remind the species of the species. I am Lucien Percival Smith. And without me, without my shattered crippled brain, you will never again be frightened by what you might have become. Or indeed, by what your future might make you. *(Lucien finishes and sits. For Jack and Senator Clarke, no time has elapsed. The lights return.)*

CLARKE. Lucien? Just one other question. Do you feel you could work outside of the sheltered workshop at the Center?

JACK. *(Seeing Lucien's confusion.)* What do you think, Lucien?

LUCIEN. Lucien P. Smith says it's hard.

CLARKE. Thank you, Lucien.

LUCIEN. *(Standing, showing the gallery.)* I got a library card. It's green. It's got my name. Lucien P. Smith. It's green. I mean business! *(The Senate goes to black. Early evening in the apartment. Norman emerges from the refrigerator with a platter on which are maybe two dozen doughnuts. He places them invitingly on the coffee table. He admires the doughnuts, then returns to the refrigerator and gets yet another platter. He joins these with the others so that there are two mounds of doughnuts on the table. The doorbell rings. For a moment, Norman is panicked. He checks his clothes, his keys. He pats down his already wet and plastered hair. Finally prepared, he goes to the door and opens it. Sheila stands*

there. She wears her best outfit. She carries a bouquet of wild-flowers. She smiles.)
NORMAN. Hi, Sheila.
SHEILA. Hi, Norman.
NORMAN. Hi, Sheila.
SHEILA. Hi, Norman.
NORMAN. Hi, Sheila. My name is Norman Bulansky. Welcome to my home. Won't you take a seat? (*Sheila enters. She stands with the flowers and looks about.*)
SHEILA. This is nice, Norman. It's cozy.
NORMAN. It used to be better when we had those little rugs. Arnold's got them hid.
SHEILA. Arnold, ick! He's not here, is he?
NORMAN. Oh boy, that's all we need. Oh boy!
SHEILA. Arnold, ick!
NORMAN. Oh boy! (*Pause.*) Can I manage your coat?
SHEILA. I don't have one.
NORMAN. Oh boy!
SHEILA. I got to leave at nine. The bus comes then. It's seven-thirty now.
NORMAN. (*With a kitchen timer.*) See this? It's a timer. It times things. Eggs and . . . eggs, and things. I'll just set it and then you won't be late.
SHEILA. It's seven-thirty now. I got to leave at nine.
NORMAN. All I do is set it like this. On the nine. See? Don't worry. This works like a butler or somebody. (*Carefully placing it down.*) My name is Norman Bulansky. Won't you take a seat?
SHEILA. I got these for you. I picked them.
NORMAN. (*Taking the flowers, pleased.*) You're welcome very much. They're pretty. You're welcome, thank you. Thank you.
SHEILA. I picked them in that lot near the Getty station. You know that lot?
NORMAN. Getty gas. That's good gas. Would you please like a doughnut?
SHEILA. You got a jar or something to put them in?
NORMAN. (*Studying the doughnuts, mystified.*) I got them on plates. In piles. See. They won't fit in a jar.

SHEILA. Gee, Norman, you're silly. I mean the flowers.

NORMAN. The flowers? Oh boy, I thought you wanted a jar for the doughnuts. Oh boy, I'm sure silly. You ain't kiddin', oh boy! (*They both laugh. Pause.*) Would you please like a doughnut?

SHEILA. I got to go at nine. The bus comes then.

NORMAN. Maybe I'll have one, thank you. (*Takes one, chomps.*) They call this one honey-dipped. But you know what? It's not real honey. I told Arnold that and he said we should picket.

SHEILA. Maybe we should put them in a jar or something.

NORMAN. I'll get a jar or something. (*Norman places the flowers on the couch, then starts for the kitchen, but is distracted.*)

SHEILA. This is nice, Norman. Real cozy. We don't have stuff on the wall in our home. We used to, but Helen with the tic eats paper sometime. It's awful.

NORMAN. Oh boy, you bet.

SHEILA. She ate a picture of God one day. God and His friends eating. She just ate it. We still got the frame, but God's all eaten up.

NORMAN. God? She ate a picture of God? Oh boy!

SHEILA. One time, Helen ate a roll of toilet paper.

NORMAN. Want to see the bathroom? We got a nice bathroom.

SHEILA. No thank you. I went before.

NORMAN. (*One last shot.*) We got swans in there.

SHEILA. (*After a pause.*) This is nice, Norman. It's cozy.

NORMAN. We used to have this poster with kitties on it, but Jack said it was too baby. I kind of liked it though. Would you please like a doughnut? (*Norman sits on the couch, crushing the flowers. He realizes what he has done. A very nervous pause. To himself.*) Oh-oh. Oh boy, oh-oh. Oh-oh . . . (*An agonized moment.*) Sheila, are the flowers under me? Do you remember?

SHEILA. I got them in that lot near the Getty station.

NORMAN. That's good gas. Getty gas. (*Gets up, sees the flowers.*) Sheila, I think somebody sat on these. I think I'm very sorry but I was just sitting down to have a doughnut and for us to talk.

SHEILA. (*Unconcerned.*) That's okay, Norman.

NORMAN. But they're all broken.

SHEILA. Flowers grow right back.

NORMAN. (*Stuffing the flowers in his pocket.*) I feel awful bad about them, Sheila.

SHEILA. That's okay, Norman, flowers break a lot. That's how come you get them free.

NORMAN. (*His pockets stuffed.*) Would you please like a doughnut?

SHEILA. I had spaghetti for supper. (*Pause. Suddenly Norman gets an idea and rushes to the refrigerator. He opens the freezer and pulls out a present: a doughnut box with maybe thirty stick-on bows attached. He gives it to her.*)

NORMAN. Sheila, I got you this. It's a present. Can I have the bows?

SHEILA. No. They're pretty. I want them.

NORMAN. Open it.

SHEILA. (*Opening it.*) Oh, Norman, I feel all jumpy.

NORMAN. Me too. Can I have the bows?

SHEILA. No. (*Pulls out a large clump of newspaper packing.*) I know what's in it. Let me guess. A frog.

NORMAN. Nope. Oh boy, a frog'd be hard to wrap.

SHEILA. Gee, Norman, you're funny.

NORMAN. I am? Oh boy, you ain't kiddin', oh boy!

SHEILA. (*Giggling.*) You are, Norman. You're funny.

NORMAN. Oh boy! (*Sheila unwraps a set of keys, smaller, but similar to his.*)

SHEILA. Oh, Norman. Keys. You got me keys. Oh, Norman . . . (*Sheila, very affected, is at a loss. Norman beams.*)

NORMAN. They're nice, huh? Try them on. Oh boy, I can't wait to see them on.

SHEILA. Norman, this is the best present I ever got.

NORMAN. Try them on. Put them on your belt. They'll fit good.

SHEILA. (*Looping the keys on her belt.*) What side?

NORMAN. Whatever makes you feel more balanced. Jack, he got me the ring. It's made of metal. And Arnold got me all the keys. He says that the movie theatre has all keys around that nobody uses too much. And Lucien, he gave me that little bitty key. It's from this diary he got, but he can't write so who cares?

SHEILA. (*Stunned with her good fortune.*) They're the most

beautiful keys I ever saw.

NORMAN. They should be. They're right from the movies. *(The kitchen timer rings. Panic strikes them both. Norman shuts it off.)* Oh boy! Did that go fast! Oh boy!

SHEILA. I got to go. I got to go for the bus at nine.

NORMAN. Seven-thirty and nine are too soon together, oh boy!

SHEILA. *(Gathering the bows and the box and the crumpled newspaper.)* I got to go, Norman.

NORMAN. A butler couldn't tell you better time. Would you please like a doughnut?

SHEILA. The bus goes at nine. It don't wait.

NORMAN. My name is Norman Bulansky. Welcome to my home. Thank you for visiting with me. *(Pulling the flowers from his pockets.)* I'm sorry I broke your flowers. Come again.

SHEILA. *(Kissing him on the cheek.)* Norman, this is the most best beautiful present I ever got.

NORMAN. *(Overwhelmed.)* Welcome to Norman Bulansky. Come again.

SHEILA. I got to go. The bus goes at nine. Bye, Norman.

NORMAN. Bye, Sheila. Thank you for visiting with me. Come again.

SHEILA. Bye. *(Sheila exits. Norman is beside himself. He discovers the broken flowers in his hands. He smells them. Swoon. He hurries to the window and opens it.)*

NORMAN. *(Yelling out.)* Sheila! Come again! Welcome to my home! (He moves from the window, beaming. He places the flowers down gently. A "great idea" strikes him. He runs to the coffee table and gets a platter of doughnuts. He returns to the window and throws all the doughnuts out, followed by the platter.)* Free doughnuts! Free doughnuts! Free doughnuts! *(The lights go to black in the apartment. Arnold enters, pushing the grocery cart. The same inexplicable shrub is in the cart.)*

ARNOLD. *(To the audience.)* I'm in a little bit of trouble with Mr. Corbin, He says if I don't bring the keys back, I'm fired. Boy, talk about Russia! So I put it down on my pad of things to do to ask Sheila. Just thinking about it gives me arthritis. *(The lights fade, and switch to a room at the institution. Barry, in*

drab institutional clothing, sits upright on a small unmade bed.
He is motionless. Jack stands watching him.)
JACK. Hi, Barry. It's me, Jack. How you doing? (*No re-*
sponse.) I picked up a book for you. Some golf tips from Jack
Nicklaus. I looked it over. It's pretty good. Lots of drawings,
lots of . . . (*Jack stops, unable to continue the charade. He*
places the book on the bed.) Maybe you can look it over later.
(*Pause.*) Norman says hello. He sent over some doughnuts,
but the doctors said they had too much sugar. Arnold finally
put the rugs back. He screamed at all of us that he wasn't a
camel and that was the end of it. You know how he is. (*With*
difficulty.) Lucien wanted me to give you this. (*Holding up a*
quarter.) It's a quarter. He says when you get out, he wants
you to give him a golf lesson. (*Nothing. Jack turns to the audi-*
ence.) When I found out about Barry's father coming, I went
to my boss and asked him to stop it. He agreed. His boss,
however, said we shouldn't interfere. He'd met Barry, he
said. Barry was stable. "Christ," he said, "not a month ago
the two of us had quite a cogent conversation." "About
what?" my boss asked. "Golf," his boss said. (*Pause.*) And
Lucien, through the machinations of Senator Clarke and his
colleagues, is once again a ward of the state. So any of you
who don't believe in Spiderman, think again. (*Pause.*) I ran
into my ex-wife again. She and her car are both still looking
great. (*Pause.*) I've finally gotten another job. Through an
old college friend, I've wrangled a position with a travel
agency. It sounds kind of . . . glamorous. I start in a couple
of weeks. (*Pause.*) I'll miss these guys. They're throwing a
surprise party for me tomorrow night. Some surprise.
Lucien told me twice. Norman told me three times. And
Arnold, the concocter of this top secret scheme, informed
me straight out that if I wanted balloons or noisemakers, I'd
have to pick them up myself. He was just too busy. I repeat,
too busy. (*A final moment.*) You see, the problem is that they
never change. I change, my life changes, my crises change.
But they stay the same. Arnold is Arnold and Norman is
Norman and Lucien is Lucien and keys are keys and doughnuts are doughnuts. (*Jack returns to Barry.*) So I just figured
I'd drop by and say hello. (*Long pause.*) Well, I . . . I'd
better get going. (*One final look.*) Don't take any wooden

nickels. (*Jack exits. Barry sits motionless. The lights go to black and come up on the apartment. A flurry of activity. Arnold is the ringleader. Inexplicably, he wears a Panama hat. Norman is busily putting plates of doughnuts here and there. Lucien, wearing his suit with a T-shirt, is spraying with an aerosol can. Couch, walls, floors, everywhere.*)

ARNOLD. Everybody do their jobs or Jack'll be here and our surprise party will be about as surprising as neuralgia.

NORMAN. The worst thing you can do is go to a party and everywhere you look there ain't no doughnuts. Oh boy, and they call it a party.

ARNOLD. Lucien, if you don't stop spraying, we're all gonna catch asthma and die.

LUCIEN. I be making it smell clean.

ARNOLD. (*Taking the aerosol.*) Lucien, this is furniture polish. You don't use this to freshen the air. This is for polishing furniture.

NORMAN. It's like flowers.

ARNOLD. Lucien, put this away! My nose smells like a bureau.

LUCIEN. (*Reluctantly putting it away.*) We be having furniture, Arnold.

ARNOLD. Norman, you said you were gonna get snacks. All I see are doughnuts.

NORMAN. Doughnuts are snacks.

ARNOLD. Doughnuts are not snacks.

NORMAN. Doughnuts are snacks.

ARNOLD. Doughnuts are not snacks.

NORMAN. Doughnuts are snacks.

ARNOLD. Doughnuts are not snacks.

LUCIEN. I hear somebody! I hear them!

ARNOLD. Quick! Shut off the lights! The lights, Lucien, the lights. Ssshhh!!! (*Lucien shuts off the lights. The men hide. The doorbell rings.*)

NORMAN. Hello. My name is Norman Bulansky. Welcome to . . .

ARNOLD. Ssshhh! (*Ultra-casually.*) Oh, come in! It's open! (*The front door opens. The men explode with enthusiasm.*)

THE MEN. (*Together.*) Surprise! Surprise! Surprise!

ARNOLD. Get the lights, Lucien!

THE MEN. (*Together.*) Surprise! Surprise!!! (*Lucien turns on the lights. Sheila stands in the doorway. She wears her keys. She is flattered by the attention. She carries a bouquet of wildflowers.*)

ARNOLD. I don't believe this.

NORMAN. (*Delighted.*) It's Sheila. Hi, Sheila. My name is Norman Bulansky. Welcome to my home. Won't you take a seat?

ARNOLD. You make a plan, you work it out, you turn out the lights, I don't believe this . . .

SHEILA. Hi, Norman.

NORMAN. Hi, Sheila.

SHEILA. Hi, Norman.

NORMAN. Hi, Sheila.

ARNOLD. I could get angina just standing here.

LUCIEN. Hi, Sheila.

SHEILA. Hi, Lucien. I got you some flowers at the Getty gas place, Norman.

NORMAN. Getty gas. That's good gas. (*Taking the flowers.*) Oh boy, they're real pretty. I hope I don't sit on them.

SHEILA. Put them up high. You can't sit on things up high.

ARNOLD. I might as well right now ask a very frank question and get it over with. Sheila, can I have your keys?

SHEILA. (*Horrified, together with Norman.*) My keys! I need my keys, Arnold! I can't get into things without my keys! I need my keys!

NORMAN. (*Together with Sheila.*) Oh boy, her keys! Her keys! Oh boy! She needs her keys! She can't get into things without her keys! Oh boy!

ARNOLD. I can see you're not quite ready to make up your mind. Good. I'll bring it up later.

LUCIEN. (*Takes the flowers and exiting into the bathroom.*) I'll put them in the tub. They won't go bad.

NORMAN. Want to see our bathroom, Sheila? We got a nice bathroom.

SHEILA. No, thank you. I went before.

ARNOLD. All right, I repeat, somebody in this room has more to do than talk talk talk.

SHEILA. How come you got that hat on, Arnold?

ARNOLD. This is my own personal hat which I bought from a bald man in a store, thank you. I will be right back with a

59

plan. (*Officiously, Arnold exits into his bedroom.*)

NORMAN. Oh boy, he thinks he's so smart, oh boy.

SHEILA. Mary Wentworth is all bald. When she takes her wig off she looks like outer space.

LUCIEN. (*Off, in the bathroom.*) Do flowers they float?

SHEILA. She doesn't have no eyebrows. It's weird.

NORMAN. No eyebrows? What does she do on a rainy day? (*Arnold enters from his room. He carries a large bag.*)

ARNOLD. When I got this stuff, I didn't tell the lady it was for a party of grown-up adults with their own home. I didn't want to be a bragger.

NORMAN. What's in there, Arnold?

SHEILA. Let me guess. A frog?

ARNOLD. No.

NORMAN. Doughnuts?

ARNOLD. They're both good guesses, but they are both, I repeat, both, wrong. (*Pulling hand puppets from the bag.*) Animal puppets! A whole bag of animal puppets!

NORMAN. How come?

LUCIEN. (*Off.*) They go like boats!

ARNOLD. How come is because with animal puppets, you are now three guests at a party instead of just one. (*Giving them each two puppets.*) Just put one on each hand.

NORMAN. These ain't people. These are puppets.

LUCIEN. (*Off.*) I see him! Here comes Jack!

ARNOLD. Here he comes!

NORMAN. Oh boy!

ARNOLD. Does she know the song?

NORMAN. No. We ain't had time.

ARNOLD. I could have expected this. Put a puppet on your hands and just mouth the words. (*Lucien enters from the bathroom. He is soaked.*)

LUCIEN. I got the flowers in the tub.

ARNOLD. (*Giving Lucien two puppets.*) Put these on.

LUCIEN. I got all wet.

NORMAN. I want a bear puppet. You got any bear puppets?

ARNOLD. I am finding this hard to believe, that's all, hard to believe.

SHEILA. Got any frogs?

LUCIEN. (*His puppets are fighting.*) Pow! Bang! Pow! Pow!

ARNOLD. Stop that, Lucien.

SHEILA. I'd like a frog, please.

LUCIEN. Pow! Sock! Bang!

NORMAN. I would have a bear please.

ARNOLD. Would everybody just please get familiar with his puppets and sing the song please.

LUCIEN. What song?

ARNOLD. This is an angina party. That's what this is. An angina party. (*The doorbell rings. They all freeze for a moment, then hide.*)

ARNOLD. It's him! Get ready!

NORMAN. Hello. My name is Norman . . .

ARNOLD. Ssshhh!!! (*Cheerfully.*) It's open. Please come right in! (*Jack enters. He has a cluster of helium balloons. Immediately Norman and Arnold, puppets on hands, join in song. Sheila and her puppets try gamely. Lucien throws in a phrase or two. Jack listens, touched.*)

NORMAN & ARNOLD. Surprise! (*Singing.*)

Home, home on the range!

Where the deer and the antelope play,

Where seldom is heard

A discouraging word,

And the clouds are not scary all day!*

(*Laughter. The applause and chatter of excited hand puppets.*)

SHEILA & THE BOYS. Surprise! Surprise! Surprise! (*Some hugging and hand shaking and stuff. Jack is clearly somwhat overwhelmed.*)

JACK. Thanks, everybody . . . Really, thanks. This is really terrific. Really . . . just terrific.

ARNOLD. Were you surprised, Jack? Be frank.

NORMAN. Would you like a doughnut, please?

ARNOLD. Here, Jack. Put on a puppet.

LUCIEN. Pow! Sock! Plowee! Zip!

ARNOLD. Stop that, Lucien!

LUCIEN. My puppets be fighting. (*Arnold, now in a snit, grabs Lucien's puppets, returning them to the bag.*)

ARNOLD. That's it! Curtain up! Back in the bag! I'm not

---

*See Special Note on Copyright page.

going to have a surprise party, I emphasize, with puppets fighting all over the place.

SHEILA. (*Protecting her puppets.*) My puppets are quiet.

NORMAN. My puppets are dead.

JACK. Guys, what's the surprise for?

ARNOLD. Don't you know, Jack? Boy, this is a surprise. You're leaving us. Harry in the van told us.

JACK. Right.

LUCIEN. Jack be leaving? Where Jack be leaving to?

ARNOLD. We've explained all this, Lucien. Maybe a million times. You should get an atlas.

LUCIEN. Jack, you be leaving where?

JACK. I got another job, Lucien. I'm going to be a travel agent.

LUCIEN. You be travelling, Jack?

JACK. But I'll still be working in the neighborhood. You know, that building with the big red awning on the way to the Center.

NORMAN. (*Vying for attention.*) Oh boy! Don't sit up front with the old people.

LUCIEN. We got no trees!

NORMAN. How many jobs you got now?

JACK. I'll just have the . . . one.

NORMAN. Us, right?

JACK. No. I'm going to work for this . . . travel agency. Help people, you know, get from place to place.

LUCIEN. We got no trees!

NORMAN. And then us, right?

JACK. No, Norman. I'm leaving you guys. But . . . really . . . it'll be fine. Somebody else'll come and take my place. Somebody'll always be here for you guys . . .

NORMAN. Somebody doesn't know us like you know us, Jack.

JACK. They will, Norman.

LUCIEN. Jack be leaving us where?

NORMAN. You can't leave us, Jack!

ARNOLD. Norman, you should have thought about this ten years ago!

JACK. C'mon guys, it's not like I'll never see you again.

NORMAN. You can't leave us, Jack!

LUCIEN. Jack be leaving us!

NORMAN. If you leave, Jack, I'll go on a hunger strike.

JACK. Look, Norman, listen for a second . . .

LUCIEN. (*An anguished realization.*) Jack be leaving us! Jack be leaving us! Jack be leaving us! (*Lucien fighting tears, rushes to his bedroom and exits.*)

JACK. (*Starting after him.*) Lucien . . . Lucien, come back here!

NORMAN. I won't eat nothing.

ARNOLD. I wouldn't, and I mean this frankly, Jack, quit you.

JACK. I am not quitting you, Arnold! I am not quitting any of you!

NORMAN. If you quit us, I won't eat nothing ever! I'll go on a hunger strike until I'm like a worm!

JACK. Guys, I thought this was supposed to be a party.

ARNOLD. (*Now angry.*) It is! This is an angina party!!

NORMAN. (*Grabbing the doughnuts.*) Hunger strike!! I'm on a hunger strike!!

LUCIEN. (*Off.*) We got no trees!

JACK. Guys!

NORMAN. (*Angry, throwing the doughnuts out the window.*) Free doughnuts! Free doughnuts! Free doughnuts!

ARNOLD. *Nyet* to you leaving us, Jack! *Nyet* to that!!

NORMAN. Free doughnuts!!!

ARNOLD. *Nyet*!!!

LUCIEN. (*Off.*) We got no trees!

JACK. Fellas!

NORMAN. Oh boy, it's so loud in here I need sunglasses. (*Norman exits angrily into his bedroom.*)

JACK. Arnold, listen to me for a second. Will you just listen!

ARNOLD. *Nyet! Nyet! Nyet!*

NORMAN. (*Off.*) Free doughnuts!

LUCIEN. (*Off.*) In the tub! In the tub! In the tub!

NORMAN. (*Off.*) Hunger strike!

LUCIEN. (*Off.*) We got no trees!

ARNOLD. *Nyet*!!! (*In a frenzy, Arnold exits into his bedroom. A moment of silence. Sheila who has been quietly watching all of this, approaches Jack.*)

SHEILA. This is nice. It's cozy. (*They stand quietly. A pause, and then, all together, an explosion of protestations from the various closed doors.*)

LUCIEN. We got no trees! We got no trees! We got no trees! (*Arnold comes out of his bedroom carrying his suitcase and wearing his "Russia" hat, and exits out the front door.*)

ARNOLD. *Nyet! Nyet! Nyet! Nyet! Nyet!*

NORMAN. Free doughnuts! Free Doughnuts! Free doughnuts!

JACK. (*Shouting to Arnold.*) Arnold! Arnold!!! (*The lights fade in the apartment as the cacophony goes on, and come up on the train station. A huge empty space with a bench.*)

TRAIN ANNOUNCEMENT. (*From offstage speakers.*) On track number one through the West subway: The Colonial. Stopping at Kingston, Westerly, New London, Old Saybrook, New Haven, Bridgeport, Stamford, Rye, Penn Station, New York. With continuing service to Washington D.C. All aboard! (*During the announcement, Arnold goes to the bench. He sits, his suitcase on his lap.*

ARNOLD. (*To the audience.*) And I came here to the train station and just waited for the Russia train. I studied my map for quite a while. And Russia, by the way, is no one-horse town. (*Studies the map, looks up.*) Then I kind of checked out my suitcase: my flashlight, my map, canned peaches, socks, and my comb. (*Removes the two small rugs.*) And the rugs, thank you very much. (*Pulls out a pair of shoes.*) And Melvin's shoes, thank you too. (*Lies down awkwardly.*) And I rested some. Who wants to get somewhere all tuckered out? *Nyet* to that! (*Pops up.*) But I couldn't get a wink in edgewise. This cop kept coming by and saying, "You can't sleep on these benches." "Boy, you're tellin' me," I told him. (*Sits forlornly, removes his hat and repacks his suitcase.*) And my hat, although it's perfect for Russia, is a bad climate for America. (*Gets up, circles the bench, returns.*) And frankly, I was getting a little hungry. And frankly also, nobody wanted to talk too much. (*Just sits.*) Going to Russia, and I mean this, is no picnic. (*Pause.*) And I got to wondering if maybe Lucien was crying again. Poor Lucien. He's a mental wreck. (*Long pause.*) I'm lost on my way to Russia, thank you. (*Arnold sits silently, sadly. He is a small, exhausted man in a large place. Jack appears. He watches Arnold, then approaches. Arnold looks up. A big smile.*) Hi, Jack, it's nice to see you today.

JACK. It's great to see you, Arnold.

ARNOLD. You taking a train somewhere?

JACK. No. No, I just thought I'd drop by and see if you wanted . . . some company.

ARNOLD. (*After a pause.*) Jack?

JACK. Yeah?

ARNOLD. I think maybe I'll go to Russia when they get it worked out a little better. Frankly, it's an awful long wait.

JACK. Good idea.

ARNOLD. Will you take me home? I think I forgot a few things.

JACK. Sure, Arnold.

ARNOLD. (*Suddenly, firmly.*) Jack, you shouldn't be quitting us.

JACK. I have to, Arnold.

ARNOLD. If you quit, Jack, I'll hate you.

JACK. I hope not.

ARNOLD. I will.

JACK. I really hope not.

ARNOLD. I will. (*A beat.*) Are you still quitting us?

JACK. Yes.

ARNOLD. Then fine. I hate you. Curtain up. End of subject. (*Long pause.*) Can we eat something? I'm very undernourished tonight.

JACK. We'll stop somewhere.

ARNOLD. Thanks, Jack. But I don't want to go anyplace where you have to eat a la carte. I don't like a la carte.

JACK. No a la carte. (*Silently, they get up. Arnold takes his suitcase. He stops.*)

ARNOLD. You're gonna be a travel agent now, huh, Jack?

JACK. Yeah.

ARNOLD. That's nice.

JACK. Yeah.

ARNOLD. Jack, and I emphasize this, you've got better behavior patterns than a lot of, I repeat, people.

JACK. Thanks, Arnold. You too. (*They share a laugh. Jack throws his arm around Arnold. They begin to walk* U. *Simultaneously, the train announcement begins.*)
TRAIN ANNOUNCEMENT. (*From offstage speakers.*) Now boarding on track number seven: Local service. Stopping at Boston, Montreal, Vancouver, Anchorage, Vladivostok, Irkutsk, Petropavlosk, Klemovischi, and Moscow. All aboard! (*Arnold looks back. Listens. Russia.*)

BLACKOUT.

THE END.

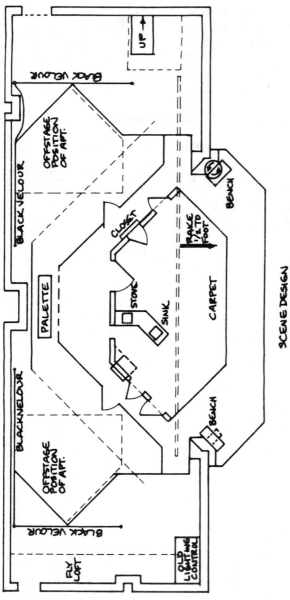

SCENE DESIGN

" THE BOYS NEXT DOOR "

BY TOM GRIFFIN
DIR. BY JOSEPHINE ABADY
AT LAMBS THEATER
DESIGNED BY DAVID POTTS

67

PROPERTY PLOT

ONSTAGE PRESET

Round kitchen table
  on: napkins in napkin holder
           sugar pourer
           salt and pepper shakers
           trivet
2 matching kitchen chairs
Small armchair
Small sofa — (cushions attached to framework)
End table
  on: 5 agriculture yearbooks stacked order from top:
           1950, 1951, 1952, 1949, 1955
Table along L. wall
  on: lamp
           ship model
Refrigerator
  in: iced tea, apple juice, American cheese, eggs, small
           bottle of seltzer
  in freezer:
           doughnut box covered with stick-on bows in:
           2 pieces of newspaper
           small set of keys
  on door:
           magnets with memos
           pictures
           dish towel
           cartoons
  on top:
           portable radio
           ball of string
           Saran wrap
           tin
  attached to side:
           broom and mop
Shelf over refrigerator
           set of cannisters
           cookie jar
Counter
  2 burner stove (not practical)

sink   (practical)
       (underneath: pressurized Hudson sprayer filled
       with water leading to hot water spigot — piping
       leading from drain into bucket with sponge to mute
       noise)
on:
       pair of rubber gloves
       bottle of Ivory Liquid filled with baby shampoo
       timer
       blender
       electric can opener
       fake African violet in basket
       tea kettle
       cup holder with 6 cups
       red glass with utensils
       dish drainer
in: 4 plates, 4 cups, 4 saucers, 2 cups
       dishwashing sponge on stick
on side: children's paintings
          straw placemats
          3 straw trivets
Wastebasket
  in: trash bag
       umbrella stand
  in: 4 umbrellas
Expanding coatrack
on: hats
4 grocery bags D.C.
  1) R. of C.
      in: 4 boxes of Wheaties
  2) R. of C.
      in: 5 boxes of Wheaties (top box upside down)
  3) L. of C.
      in: bag of charcoal briquets, grocery receipt, quart
      of milk
  4) L. of C.
      in: 7 heads of iceburg lettuce
2 open kid's Band-Aids open behind bathroom door
Step unit in place under U.C. door
Dance table preset U.R.

OTHER ONSTAGE DRESSING

Workwheel on closet door
Map of Asia with Russia outlined and Moscow starred on
    Arnold's door
Golf magazine pictures on Barry's door
3 nightlights
Ship's wheel wall lamp
Hanging plant
Fire extinguisher
Thermostat
Mail/message basket on the door
Interior doorbell chimes container
Van Gogh print
Wall phone
Pot holders on hook

STAGE RIGHT PRESET

Yellow Rubbermaid tub
    in: 1 1/2 " water
          2 capfuls of Mr. Bubble
Blue tub
    in: 2 or 3 inches of water (Lucien in bathtub)
2 towels
2 chairs for Senate
Bench for dance with red and pink crepe paper around legs
Laundry basket with pillow (for throwing doughnuts)
Train bench
Black makeup and wet makeup sponge (for Arnold)
Spritzer bottle (for Arnold)
    Library card   (Lucien)
    2 agriculture books — 1947, 1948   (Lucien)
    Grocery bag   (Jack)
        in: box of Wheaties
              qt. of milk
              litre of seltzer
              can of Pledge (aersol can of mineral water with
                            "Pledge" label)
        rice cakes
        can of coffee

70

Box of broken doughnut pieces	(Norman)
Golf club—driver	(Mr. Hedges)
Large metal flashlight	(Lucien)
Black and red plastic flashlight	(Norman)
Pillow in case	(Norman)
in: "rat" in pocket	
Orange	(Jack)
Wall Street Journal	(Barry)
Golf magazine	(Norman)
Letter in envelope from Mr. Klemper	(Norman)
Pair of black shoes	(Arnold)
Popcorn container	(Arnold)
in: handfuls of popcorn	
Window box	(Lucien)
in: dirt	
trowel	
small plastic box	
in: 4 tomatoes	
Green reference book	(Lucien)
Pair of white and black shoes	(Arnold)
White shoe polish	(Arnold)
2 pennies	(Lucien)
1 pair yellow rubber gloves	(Norman)
Grocery bag	(Jack)
in: pancake mix	
potatoes au gratin	
can of creamed corn	
qt. of milk	
Blue bathmat & welcome mat	(Arnold)
Large crayons	(Barry)
Cardboard box	(Jack)
in: 4 fold-up paper balls	
1 yellow fold-up flower	
Film cannister	(Mr. Corbin)
Mailing labels & marker	(Mr. Corbin)
Paper bag	(Mr. Klemper)
in: broken "chocolate heart" wrapped	
in red cellophane	
Pair of cowboy boots	(Arnold)
Shoe brush	(Arnold)

Shopping cart   (Arnold)
   in: white and black shoes
         cowboy boots
         bathmat
         welcome mat
         shrub
Paper bag   (Arnold)
   in: 10 hand puppets
Red suitcase   (Arnold)
   in: map of Russia, can of peaches, pair of socks,
         flashlight, comb, blue bathmat, white and black
         shoes

STAGE LEFT PRESET

Blue-covered dance tabletop
   with: blue, red and yellow plastic cups
           6 – 8 glass punch cups
           punch bowl with ladle
           in: punch
                 2 2-litre bottles of Slice
                 2 2-litre bottles of Pepsi
                 bowl of popcorn
                 4 silver mylar balloons with jelly bean weights
Library ladder
Doiley, 2 glasses and silver pitcher
Knitting bag. . . . .(Mrs. Fremus)
   in: knitting
Pocket calculator. . . . .(Barry)
Metal flashlight. . . . .(Arnold)
Aluminum bowl worn as hat. . . . .(Arnold)
Shopping cart. . . . . (Arnold)
   in: shrub
Five-iron golf club. . . . . (Mrs. Fremus)
Poster board. . . . . (Barry)
       Barry makes golf poster new each night
Handful of buttons. . . . . (Lucien)
Bowl of popcorn. . . . .(Clara)
Pink rubber gloves. . . . .(Arnold
4 sanitary napkins. . . . . (Arnold)
Toilet brush. . . . . (Arnold)

Roll of 1″ masking tape. . . . . (Barry)
Welcome Home Dad sign. . . . . (Barry)
Five-iron golf club. . . . . (Barry)
Suede folder with pad. . . . . (Sen. Clarke)
Bouquet of daisies. . . . . (Sheila)
Wrapped golf book. . . . . (Jack)
Quarter. . . . . (Jack)
Bouquet of daisies. . . . . (Sheila)
4 colored balloons with jelly bean weights. . . . . . (Jack)

PERSONAL PROPS

Norman	Large hook-on key ring with lots of keys
Arnold	Pocket notebook
	Pencil
Barry	Golf ball
	Golf tees
Jack	Paperback copy of *A Tale of Two Cities*

COSTUME PLOT

JACK PALMER

Opening Scene:
Khaki pleated trousers
Light brown woven-look belt
Burnt orange gabardine shirt
Dark blue socks
Brown moccasins
Watch with grosgrain band

Railroad Tracks:
Blue jeans
Black three-button pullover knit shirt
Same socks, shoes, watch

Pre-Dance and Dance
Blue jeans
Blue chambray shirt
Light brown woven-look belt
Maroon vintage tie
Tan penny loafer shoes
Same socks and watch
Navy blue blazer

Housecleaning Scene:
Khaki pleated pants
Light brown woven-look belt
Black three-button pullover knit sirt
Brown moccasins
Watch

Uncle Roland Monologue:
Blue jeans
Navy blue sportcoat
Gabardine plaid shirt
Watch, socks, tan belt
Shoes

Mr. Klemper Scene:
Pleated khaki pants
Burnt orange gabardine shirt

Light tan woven-look belt
Same socks, shoes, watch

State Senate: (QUICK CHANGE FROM MR. KLEMPER
SCENE)
Navy blue blazer
Dress khaki trousers
Pale blue and white striped shirt
Tan woven-look belt
Blue foulard print tie
Penny loafers
Same socks, watch

Institution:
Blue jeans
Plaid gabardine shirt
Penny loafers
Same socks and watch

Surprise Party and Train Station:
Blue jeans
Tan belt
Blue chambray shirt
Brown moccasins
Socks, watch

GENERAL NOTE: WHENEVER WITHOUT JACKET,
SHIRTSLEEVES ARE ROLLED UP

ARNOLD WIGGINS

Glasses with red, white and blue elastic band worn
    throughout
Always has pocket-protector with pens and pencils

Opening Scene:
Pale green plaid shirt
Tan plaid pants
Brown belt
T-shirt
Blue baseball cap
Orange suede lace-up shoes
White socks with striped tops

Rat Scene:
Red, white and blue striped short pajamas
Brown house slippers
Same socks

Shopping Cart Cross:
Same as Opening Scene

Movie Theatre Scene:
Green coveralls with "Bob" name tag (can be worn over
    other clothes as necessary)
Blue cap
Orange suede shoes
White striped socks

Act I Dance Scene:
Blue and tan poly checked sport coat
Elastic waist yellow ochre trousers
Off-white, key pattern shirt
Yellow, red, blue striped tie
Orange suede shoes
White striped socks
N.B.: pants sprayed wet offstage for second entrance

Act II Movie Theatre:
Coveralls, cap, shoes, socks as in previous movie theatre
    scene

Housecleaning Scene:
(underdress under previous scene)
Green gym shorts
Brown geometric print shirt
T-shirt
Brown work gloves
Brown house slippers
White striped socks

Mr. Corbin Scene:
Same as Movie Theatre scene

Movie Theatre:
Same as above

Shopping Cart Cross:
Same as above

Surprise Party:
Repeat Dance scene without sport coat
Panama hat

Train Station:
Same as Surprise Party without panama hat
Black fur "Russia" hat

NORMAN BULANSKY

Opening Scene:
Doughnut shop shirt
T-shirt
Black polyester pants
Doughnut shop hat
Black plastic watch
Black belt with large ring of keys (props)
Black lace-up shoes
Navy blue reindeer socks

Rat Scene:
T-shirt
Off-white print boxer shorts
Navy blue reindeer socks
Black belt with keys

Mrs. Warren Scene:
Same as Opening

Dance Scene:
Doughnut shop shirt
Blue and yellow striped necktie
T-shirt
Houndstooth checked pants
Black belt with keys
Black lace-up shoes
Blue reindeer socks
Black plastic watch

Housecleaning:
T-shirt
Reddish button-down shirt
Orangish polyknit distressed pants
Black belt with keys

77

Black lace-up shoes
Blue reindeer socks
Black plastic watch

Dance Scene- Act II:
Doughnut shop shirt
T-shirt
Blue and yellow stripe tie
Brown knit pants
Black lace-up shoes
Navy blue reindeer socks
Black belt with keys
Black plastic watch

Date:
Brown and white plaid shirt
T-shirt
Brown knit pants
Pinkish striped tie
Belt with keys
Shoes, socks, watch as before

Surprise Party:
Brown and white plaid shirt
T-shirt
Houndstooth checked pants
Yellow and blue striped tie
Belt with keys
Shoes, socks, watch as before

BARRY KLEMPER

White golf glove (always in pocket or worn)

Mr. Hedges Scene:
Burgundy nylon windbreaker
Blue sweatpants
Green and red striped cotton-knit shirt
Grey sneakers
Athletic socks with 3 wide bands of color
Madras patchwork golf cap
Plaid handkerchief
Large gold watch with stretch band

Mrs. Fremus I Scene:
Same as above

Rat Scene:
Same as above

Mrs. Warren Scene:
Same as above except
Multi-colored stripe cotton-knit shirt
Dark blue striped socks

Mrs. Fremus II scene:
Same as above

Gardening Scene:
Same as above

Housecleaning Scene:
Same as above except
Green and white large striped cotton knit shirt
Either pair of socks

Mr. Klemper scene:
Madras patchwork trousers
Burgundy elastic belt
Yellow knit shirt
White golf cleat shoes
Bright green socks
Same golf cap, watch

Institution:
Grey institutional uniform pajamas
Plastic hospital I.D. bracelet

LUCIEN P. SMITH

Opening:
White with blue striped shirt
Grey pleated trousers
Green and red clip on suspenders
Rust colored lace-up shoes
Tan with small pattern socks

Rat Scene:
Flannel pajamas

Mrs. Warren Scene:
Pajamas
Black and red plaid bathrobe
Brown corduroy slippers

Pre-dance:
Same as above

Gardening Scene:
Same as above plus
Gold wool and suede sweater
Baseball cap

Library:
Same as Opening
Baseball cap

Housecleaning:
Same as Opening

State Senate:
Two-piece grey suit with suspenders
White short sleeve shirt
Grey tie with "Spiderman"
Rust colored shoes
Tan socks

Surprise Party:
Trousers from grey suit
Pajama top
Suspenders
Spiderman tie
Rust colored shoes
Tan socks

SHEILA

Zip-up body padding
Black plastic "computer style" watch
Fake "bangs" with headband

Dance:
Blue pleated poly knit skirt
White half slip

White floral print blouse
Tortoise headband
Tan thick-soled strap shoes
Orange cotton socks

Clara Scene:
Teal green poly pull-on slacks
Multi-colored striped pullover blouse
String around neck with Crackerjack box prizes
Tortoise headband
Tan oxfords
Orange cotton socks

Date:
Orange and white plaid skirt
Green elastic belt with attached change purse
White half slip
Orange-striped pullover shirt
Things on string around neck
Tan lace-up oxfords
Blue socks
Yellow headband

Surprise Party:
Blue pleated poly knit skirt
White half slip
Multi-colored striped shirt
String with things around neck
Tan lace-up oxfords
Blue socks
Green elastic belt with attached chain purse and prop keys
Yellow headband with pre-made bow

MR. KLEMPER:

Two-piece dark grey glen plaid suit with pressed-in wrinkles
Black, slightly distressed belt
Tan shirt, top button open
Grey tie with small colored stripes- pressed flat (not tight at
    collar)
Black slip-on shoes
Brown nylon socks

White handkerchief
Silver pocket watch with chain
One-arm padding and ace bandage

MR. HEDGES

Ochre plaid Bermuda shorts
Brown belt
Yellow Banlon knit sport shirt
Brown wing tip shoes
Dark blue socks
Gold wedding band
Pale blue slouch hat with plaid band

MR. CORBIN

Brown vest and trousers (from three-piece suit)
Brown belt
White, rust, grey muted plaid shirt — sleeves rolled up, top
   button open
Olive tie with gold stripe- loose
Brown tasseled loafers
Dark blue socks
Gold wedding band
Silver watch
Brown fedora
T-shirt

SENATOR CLARKE

Grey/blue pinstripe three-piece suit
White on white stripes
Red, white, blue rep stripe tie
Off-white, burgundy and green suspenders
Black lace-up shoes
White pocket square
Gold with brown leather band watch
T-shirt
Gold tie clip
Gold wedding band
Dark blue socks

MRS. FREMUS

First Scene:
Wig
Floral print with brown overtone dress
Off-white full slip
Shoes
Sweater
Narrow gold band watch
Pink framed glasses on bead chain
Yellow gold wedding band
Handkerchief

Second Scene:
Same as first scene except
Dark floral print dress with gold brooch
Bead clip on earrings

MRS. WARREN

Wig
Turquoise skirt with coordinating blouse
White half slip
Tan penny loafers
Stockings
Gold stretch band watch
Small gold earrings
"Diamond" ring
Gold wedding band

CLARA

Navy blue poly knit pants
Yellow floral shirt with floral smock
Black lace-up shoes with patent leather trim
White cotton socks

NEW PLAYS

- **MERE MORTALS** by David Ives, author of *All in the Timing*. Another critically acclaimed evening of one-act comedies combining wit, satire, hilarity and intellect -- a winning combination. The entire evening of plays can be performed by 3 men and 3 women. ISBN: 0-8222-1632-9

- **BALLAD OF YACHIYO** by Philip Kan Gotanda. A provocative play about innocence, passion and betrayal, set against the backdrop of a Hawaiian sugar plantation in the early 1900s. *"Gotanda's writing is superb ... a great deal of fine craftsmanship on display here, and much to enjoy."* --*Variety*. *"...one of the country's most consistently intriguing playwrights..."* --*San Francisco Examiner*. *"As he has in past plays, Gotanda defies expectations..."* --*Oakland Tribune*. [3M, 4W] ISBN: 0-8222-1547-0

- **MINUTES FROM THE BLUE ROUTE** by Tom Donaghy. While packing up a house, a family converges for a weekend of flaring tempers and shattered illusions. *"With MINUTES FROM THE BLUE ROUTE [Donaghy] succeeds not only in telling a story -- a typically American one with wide appeal, about how parents and kids struggle to understand each other and mostly fail -- but in notating it inventively, through wittily elliptical, crisscrossed speeches, and in making it carry a fairly vast amount of serious weight with surprising ease."* --*Village Voice*. [2M, 2W] ISBN: 0-8222-1608-6

- **SCAPIN** by Molière, adapted by Bill Irwin and Mark O'Donnell. This adaptation of Molière's 325-year-old farce, *Les Fourberies de Scapin*, keeps the play in period while adding a late Twentieth Century spin to the language and action. *"This SCAPIN, [with a] felicitous adaptation by Mark O'Donnell, would probably have gone over big with the same audience who first saw Molière's Fourberies de Scapin...in Paris in 1671."* --*N.Y. Times*. *"Commedia dell'arte and vaudeville have at least two things in common: baggy pants and Bill Irwin. All make for a natural fit in the celebrated clown's entirely unconventional adaptation."* --*Variety* [9M, 3W, flexible] ISBN: 0-8222-1603-5

- **THE TURN OF THE SCREW** adapted for the stage by Jeffrey Hatcher from the story by Henry James. The American master's classic tale of possession is given its most interesting "turn" yet: one woman plays the mansion's terrified governess while a single male actor plays everyone else. *"In his thoughtful adaptation of Henry James' spooky tale, Jeffrey Hatcher does away with the supernatural flummery, exchanging the story's balanced ambiguities about the nature of reality for a portrait of psychological vampirism..."* --*Boston Globe*. [1M, 1W] ISBN: 0-8222-1554-3

- **NEVILLE'S ISLAND** by Tim Firth. A middle management orientation exercise turns into an hilarious disaster when the team gets "shipwrecked" on an uninhabited island. *"NEVILLE'S ISLAND ... is that rare event: a genuinely good new play..., it's a comedic, adult LORD OF THE FLIES..."* --*The Guardian*. *"... A non-stop, whitewater deluge of comedy both sophisticated and slapstick.... Firth takes a perfect premise and shoots it to the extreme, flipping his fish out of water, watching them flop around a bit, and then masterminding the inevitable feeding frenzy."* --*New Mexican*. [4M] ISBN: 0-8222-1581-0

DRAMATISTS PLAY SERVICE, INC.
440 Park Avenue South, New York, NY 10016 212-683-8960 Fax 212-213-1539
postmaster@dramatists.com www.dramatists.com

NEW PLAYS

• **TAKING SIDES by Ronald Harwood.** Based on the true story of one of the world's greatest conductors whose wartime decision to remain in Germany brought him under the scrutiny of a U.S. Army determined to prove him a Nazi. *"A brave, wise and deeply moving play delineating the confrontation between culture, and power, between art and politics, between irresponsible freedom and responsible compromise." --London Sunday Times.* [4M, 3W] ISBN: 0-8222-1566-7

• **MISSING/KISSING by John Patrick Shanley.** Two biting short comedies, MISSING MARISA and KISSING CHRISTINE, by one of America's foremost dramatists and the Academy Award winning author of *Moonstruck.* *" ... Shanley has an unusual talent for situations ... and a sure gift for a kind of inner dialogue in which people talk their hearts as well as their minds...." --N.Y. Post.* MISSING MARISA [2M], KISSING CHRISTINE [1M, 2W] ISBN: 0-8222-1590-X

• **THE SISTERS ROSENSWEIG by Wendy Wasserstein, Pulitzer Prize-winning author of *The Heidi Chronicles.*** Winner of the 1993 Outer Critics Circle Award for Best Broadway Play. A captivating portrait of three disparate sisters reuniting after a lengthy separation on the eldest's 50th birthday. *"The laughter is all but continuous." --New Yorker. "Funny. Observant. A play with wit as well as acumen.... In dealing with social and cultural paradoxes, Ms. Wasserstein is, as always, the most astute of commentators." --N.Y. Times.* [4M, 4W] ISBN: 0-8222-1348-6

• **MASTER CLASS by Terrence McNally. Winner of the 1996 Tony Award for Best Play.** Only a year after winning the Tony Award for *Love! Valour! Compassion!,* Terrence McNally scores again with the most celebrated play of the year, an unforgettable portrait of Maria Callas, our century's greatest opera diva. *"One of the white-hot moments of contemporary theatre. A total triumph." --N.Y. Post. "Blazingly theatrical." -- USA Today.* [3M, 3W] ISBN: 0-8222-1521-7

• **DEALER'S CHOICE by Patrick Marber.** A weekly poker game pits a son addicted to gambling against his own father, who also has a problem but won't admit it. *"... make tracks to DEALER'S CHOICE, Patrick Marber's wonderfully masculine, razor-sharp dissection of poker-as-life.... It's a play that comes out swinging and never lets up -- a witty, wisecracking drama that relentlessly probes the tortured souls of its six very distinctive ... characters. CHOICE is a cutthroat pleasure that you won't want to miss." --Time Out (New York).* [6M] ISBN: 0-8222-1616-7

• **RIFF RAFF by Laurence Fishburne.** RIFF RAFF marks the playwriting debut of one of Hollywood's most exciting and versatile actors. *"Mr. Fishburne is surprisingly and effectively understated, with scalding bubbles of anxiety breaking through the surface of a numbed calm." --N.Y. Times. "Fishburne has a talent and a quality...[he] possesses one of the vital requirements of a playwright -- a good ear for the things people say and the way they say them." --N.Y. Post.* [3M] ISBN: 0-8222-1545-4

DRAMATISTS PLAY SERVICE, INC.
440 Park Avenue South, New York, NY 10016 212-683-8960 Fax 212-213-1539
postmaster@dramatists.com www.dramatists.com